BIG BOOK

OF

GAMES AND ACTIVITIES FOR YOUNG CHILDREN

Gospel Light

HOW TO MAKE CLEAN COPIES FROM THIS BOOK

You may make copies of portions of this book with a clean conscience if

- you (or someone in your organization) are the original purchaser;

- you are using the copies you make for a noncommercial purpose (such as teaching or promoting your ministry) within your church or organization;

- you follow the instructions provided in this book.

However, it is ILLEGAL for you to make copies if

- you are using the material to promote, advertise or sell a product or service other than for ministry fund-raising;

- you are using the material in or on a product for sale; or

- you or your organization are not the original purchaser of this book.

By following these guidelines you help us keep our products affordable.

Thank you,
Gospel Light

Editorial Staff

Founder, Henrietta Mears
Publisher Emeritus, William T. Greig
Publisher, Children's Curriculum and Resources, Lynnette Pennings, M.A.
Senior Consulting Publisher, Dr. Elmer L. Towns
Managing Editor, Sheryl Haystead
Senior Consulting Editor, Wesley Haystead, M.S.Ed.
Senior Editor, Biblical and Theological Issues, Bayard Taylor, M.Div.
Editorial Team, Rachel Hong, Benjamin Unseth
Contributing Editors, Mandy Abbas, Carol Eide, Lea Fowler, Mary Mleziva
Designer, Zelle Olson

How to Use This Book

HOW Can These Games and Activities Be Used?

This book offers hundreds of games and activities which you can use for fun and Bible learning with young children at church or at home. Cut apart and use these reproducible pages as they are, or photocopy them for use with large groups or for multiple use. These games and activities require only minor preparation, and most require no other material than what is provided in this book. Read the brief easy-to-follow instructions, photocopy a page or two, and you and your children will be ready to play. As children play, be available to guide them through learning a new activity and to encourage their interaction and achievement through your conversation.

To connect the games and activities to Bible stories and verses, look through the contents pages and find games and activities which will supplement and enrich the Bible story your children are learning. For example, if your children are learning about creation or Noah's ark, they could play:

- Charades, using a set of animal cards from the Card Games section
- Animal Race or Animals Everywhere from the Board Games section
- Mosaic, using dominoes from the Domino Play section to create their own animal or creation pictures

Children would also enjoy:

- acting out the Bible story, using people, animals and even a Noah's Ark puppet from the Puppets section
- illustrating the Bible story, using the Garden, the Forest or the Mountain Meadow from the Play Scenes section

If you are teaching a verse such as "Love one another" (John 13:34), choose any game from the book. Talk about ways of showing love and kindness to each other as the game is played.

WHO Are These Games and Activities Planned For?

All of these games and activities are intended for young children (three to seven years old) at

- Sunday School
- Children's Church
- Vacation Bible School
- Preschool
- Day school
- Child care
- Home
- Kindergarten
- Birthday parties
- Places where children must sit quietly and wait (at a doctor's office, in a car, at a workplace, etc.)

WHY Use the Games and Activities?

Children enjoy the challenge of learning new skills and information—if these things are presented in an interesting way and within each child's understanding and physical abilities. Children are here-and-now people, and these games and activities involve children immediately. The Big Book of Games and Activities for Young Children includes a variety of opportunities for children to learn through some of their God-given senses: hearing, seeing, touching.

Here's the best part of these games and activities from the children's viewpoint: The activities are FUN! Enjoy these activities with the children you guide. Add a smile to your words. If you're happy and enthusiastic, then the children will reflect your joy.

HOW to Prepare the Games and Activities

Card Games, Board Games, Domino Play

☼ Photocopy the pages onto white and/or colored card stock or copier paper (see a game's Preparation instructions for any specifications).

☼ Laminate pages or cover with clear Con-Tact paper.

☼ Cut pages apart along the heavy lines using a paper cutter or scissors.

☼ For a handy collection of games and activities, save each set of prepared materials with a copy of the game and its directions in an envelope, folder or resealable plastic bag.

Puppet Activities

☼ Photocopy puppets (pp. 157-197).

☼ Cut pages apart along the heavy lines using a paper cutter or scissors.

☼ Prefold puppets.

☼ For a handy collection of puppets, save puppets and a copy of the activity directions in an envelope, folder or resealable plastic bag.

Play Scenes

☼ Photocopy pages (pp. 203-233) onto white copier paper or card stock.

☼ Each page goes with another page to form a two-page scene. The first page of each of these pairs is marked as the "Left page" and the second as the "Right page." First allow the children to color the pages. Then tape pages together.

☼ For a handy collection of scenes, save each page with a copy of the activity directions in an envelope, folder or resealable plastic bag.

Contents

Children enjoy surprises, learning, the feeling of achievement and time spent with others while playing games. These games make all this possible because they are designed for a young child's interests and abilities. Rules for some traditional games have been simplified. The game cards picture things young children love and are eager to play with. Each set of game cards can be used with a variety of games.

Board Games. 103

Children will experience a tremendous variety of play and activity with these delightful new games. Sometimes young children will be hopping, sometimes building, sometimes matching—and always having fun! All the resources for these games are right here in the book.

Games. 105

Game Boards 111

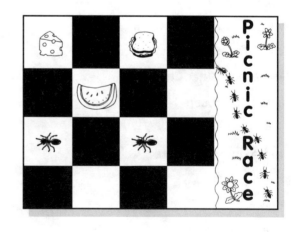

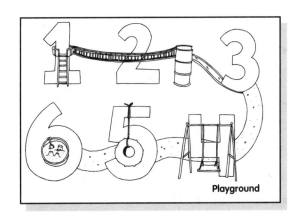

Playground

Puppet Activities 151

Children will love playing—and learning—with these puppets. The versatile and easy-to-use puppets include people, animals and even child and adult vehicles. The suggested activities will allow you to effectively use puppets in any lesson or as free play.

Activities 153

Puppets 157

Play Scenes 199

Children can use these scenes to act out favorite Bible stories or contemporary situations. This can be done either with the puppets from the preceding section or with toys. These scenes are also ready to use for creative art and nature activities. The scenes can even be enlarged so that children can create hands-on wall murals.

Activities 201

Domino Play 235

Children love dominoes, but traditional dominoes require significant math skills and pattern recognition abilities and come in large sets. The games and sets in this book fit young children: there are fewer dominoes than in regular sets, and pattern recognition is by looking at pictures rather than by counting a number of figures. The activity list includes teamwork games and open-ended creative activities which offer fun possibilities for each of your children.

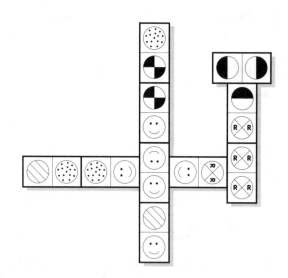

Age-Level Characteristics of Young Children

3s

Physical

The three-year-old child is in constant movement. The child tumbles often. Large muscles are developing, but small hand and finger muscles are not developed. Threes may build structures with blocks, draw pictures which they will name as objects or people, begin to count and may begin to use scissors on heavy straight lines. Activities involving puppets also provide opportunities for movement.

Teaching Tips: Plan for freedom of movement. Choose movement-oriented games such as Hide and Seek and Playground. Young children will enjoy stretching, stepping, jumping and clapping.

Mental/Emotional

Three-year-olds have short attention spans. They are beginning to recognize their name in print. Three-year-olds are explorers; they learn through their senses. They will enjoy the games and activities because they are based on pictures and most require no math or reading skills.

Teaching Tips: When telling children what to do in a game, give one brief direction at a time. Wait patiently until they have responded before you continue with the next direction. Young children will learn a game through repetition. And unlike adults, they will enjoy a game more and more as they repeat it.

Social

Threes can interact in play with others. However, it's still a "ME, MY, MINE" world. Sharing and taking turns is hard to do. When a conflict arises, children respond better to distraction than to reasoning.

Teaching Tips: Kindness and patience are necessary. Offer opportunities for play with other children. Know each child as an individual and use his or her name often. Help each child to succeed by providing activities appropriate for the child's abilities.

Spiritual

The three-year-old can learn that God made all things and that God cares for him or her; that Jesus is God's Son and that He did kind, loving things when He lived on Earth; that the Bible is a special book about God and Jesus and that Bible stories are true.

Teaching Tips: The child's learning about God is dependent on not only what people say but also what people show about God. Your loving actions help the child understand God's love. Help the child experience God's presence in our world through a variety of seeing, touching, smelling, tasting and hearing activities. Talk and sing about God.

4s and 5s

Physical

At this age children are in a period of rapid physical growth. Coordination is greatly improved. These children are still constantly on the move—running, jumping, walking or climbing—and need open spaces to move about freely! Girls often mature more rapidly than boys.

Teaching Tips: Because children at this age are gaining control of small muscles, provide activities that involve fine coordination. The rapid growth and constant activity of the child easily causes fatigue, so alternate times of active and quiet activity.

Mental/Emotional

Fours and fives are curious and questioning. They may concentrate for longer periods, but their attention span is still short. Children will interpret your words literally. Fours and fives may talk accurately about recent events and pronounce most common words correctly.

Teaching Tips: Use large teaching pictures to reinforce basic concepts. Set realistic limits and emphasize the behavior you desire. ("Raymond, running is a good thing to do outside where there is lots of room. Inside we have to walk, so no one will get hurt." "Jocelyn, you may only draw on your own paper. Are there any more places on your page that you want to make purple?") Help children discover things for themselves by having the freedom to experiment (play).

Social

The four- or five-year-old child can participate with other children in group activities. The child actively seeks adult approval, responds to friendliness and wants to be loved, especially by his or her teacher. Some children may use negative ways of gaining attention from others.

Teaching Tips: Provide opportunities for group activities. Give each child individual attention before negative behavior occurs. Make eye contact often, listen carefully to the child and smile and show that the child is special to you.

Spiritual

The four- and five-year-old child can learn basic information about God—He made the world; He cares for all people. A child this age can also learn that Jesus is God's Son, that He lived on Earth to show God's love for us, that He died but rose again and is still alive today. Fours and fives can be taught that the Bible tells us ways to obey God and that he or she can talk to God in prayer.

Teaching Tips: Because the child still thinks literally and physically, avoid the use of symbolic words and phrases such as "born again," "open your heart" or "fishers of men." When about to use a symbolic expression, think of the simplest literal explanation you could give of what the expression means. Then use that simple explanation *instead* of the symbolic one, which may confuse the child.

6s and 7s

Physical

Young school-age children need opportunities for movement during every class session. Small muscle coordination is still developing and improving. Girls are ahead of boys at this stage of development.

Teaching Tips: Use activities that involve cutting. Give children opportunities to change positions and to move about the room. Vary the activities.

Mental/Emotional

Six- and seven-year-olds have an intense eagerness to learn. They like to repeat stories and activities. Each child thinks everyone shares his or her view. Children see parts rather than how the parts make up the whole. Children are experiencing new and frequently intense feelings as they grow in independence; sometimes they find it hard to control their behavior. There is still a deep need for approval from adults and a growing need for approval by peers.

Teaching Tips: Consider the skills and interests of the children in planning activities. For example, some can follow a game's directions well while others will enjoy a less-directed, more creative activity. Show genuine interest in each child and his or her activities and accomplishments. Learn children's names and use them frequently in positive ways.

Social

The Golden Rule is a tough concept for six- and seven-year-olds. Being first and winning are very important. Taking turns is hard. This skill improves by the end of the second grade. A child's social process moves gradually from "I" to "you" to "we."

Teaching Tips: Provide opportunities for children to practice taking turns. Help each child accept the opinions and wishes of others and consider the welfare of the group as well as his or her own. Call attention to times when the group cooperated successfully.

Spiritual

Six- and seven-year-olds can sense the greatness, wonder and love of God when helped with visual and specific examples. The nonphysical nature of God is baffling, but God's presence in every area of life is generally accepted when parents and teachers communicate this belief by their attitudes and actions. Children can think of Jesus as a friend, but they need specific examples of how Jesus expresses love and care. This understanding leads many children to belief and acceptance of Jesus as personal Savior. Children can comprehend talking to God anywhere, anytime in their own words, and need regular opportunities to pray. They can also comprehend that the Old Testament tells what happened before Jesus was born and the New Testament tells of His birth, work on Earth and return to heaven and the works that occurred afterwards on Earth.

Teaching Tips: The gospel becomes real as children feel love from adults. Teachers who demonstrate their faith in a consistent, loving way are models through which the loving nature of God is made known to children.

Classroom Discipline Tips

"What a morning this has been!" comments a bewildered teacher.

"Why can't little children sit still?" sighs another. "What these kids need is discipline!"

Why is a child's behavior sometimes puzzling and frustrating? Why *do* children "act like that"?

No two children are alike. We cannot begin to number the different experiences each child has had in the first six years of life. Nor can we fathom the varying expectations that families have placed upon these children. And yet—knowing these things—we continue to be surprised when children do not act the way we have anticipated they will act.

By the same token, no two teachers are alike. And yet most of us, when surrounded by a roomful of children, are painfully alike. We want children to *behave*—which usually means we want them to act the way we antici-pate they will act!

Where can the weary teacher find help? Is discipline the answer? And just what *is* discipline?

Allow Freedom Within Limits

Good discipline is what you do *with* and *for* a child, not what you do *to* him or her. Discipline, then, is the guid-ance an adult gives so that a child knows what he or she *may* do as well as what he or she *may not* do.

For a child to grow into a thoughtful and loving adult, he or she needs to begin developing self-control—direc-tion from within. To accomplish this lifelong task, the child needs loving and understanding adults to guide behavior until he or she is mature enough to handle the task alone.

Learning to get along with others and to creatively use materials and equipment help a child enjoy the begin-ning of his or her church school experience. A child has (we hope) many years of church attendance ahead. How important, then, that these first experiences be pleasant ones! To establish a positive learning atmosphere, there are several important points to remember.

Provide love and care for each child. This love is not the gushy kind but a love that gives a child what he or she needs to grow and develop. Children long to feel that someone cares about them, that they are peo-ple of worth and value. Demonstrate your love and care in ways a child can understand. Sit down at the child's eye level and listen attentively to what a child has to say. Kindly but firmly redirect a child's out-of-bounds activity. When you redirect a child's disruptive or unacceptable activity, do not scold or shame the child. Scolding or shaming makes the child feel excluded from your love. Focus on the child's *behavior*, not on the person. Let the child know you love him or her but that you cannot allow the mis-behavior. In all your actions and words, reflect the unconditional love you yourself have experienced from God.

Plan an interesting schedule of activities. If you expect children to sit quietly and wait for an activity to begin, then you are asking them to act like miniature adults. Normal young children often misbehave simply because they are bored. Young children need action. As they grow and learn, they *must* move around. They learn best by touching and testing everything around them. For this reason, it's best to offer a variety of activities.

Help children feel a sense of security and order. Tell them by your actions and your words that they are safe in your care and that you will allow no harm to come to them. Children also find security in knowing you are near-by to assist when they need help. When they are assured you will be there to help, they will be more willing to try a new activity or experience.

Children like to be fairly sure of what will happen next. Follow the same schedule of activities each week. Of course, there will be times when you will need to be flexible by shortening or lengthening parts of the schedule, depending on the interest and attention span of the children.

A child feels secure with limits. He or she needs to know what you expect. Establish a few basic rules such as "Crayons stay on the table." Phrase the rules in a positive way whenever you can. Help children remember and observe the rules during their work and play. Give each child consistent and positive guidance. Find a middle ground between rigid authority and total permissiveness. Children need limits, but they also need freedom to move around and make choices within those limits.

Children respond in a positive way to a neatly arranged room with fresh and interesting things to do. The same old stuff in the same old places, with pieces missing or parts broken, is almost certain to invite misbehavior.

When a child receives an adult's thoughtful and consistent guidance, he or she is on the way to understanding what it means to be responsible for one's own behavior. From this responsibility grows self-control—discipline from within.

Control Unacceptable Behavior

Sometimes a teacher's most thoughtful preparation and guidance do not keep a child from misbehaving. With most preschoolers, you have only about 10 seconds to do the correcting. Avoid long explanations. Although there are no surefire guarantees for these special situations, here are a few brief suggestions to guide you:

When a child hits (kicks, scratches)—"That hurts. I cannot let you hit Shannon. And I cannot let Shannon hit you. You may not hurt other people here. *Tell* Shannon what you want." Separate the two children. Redirect the offender's activity to another area of the room, and stay with the child until he or she is constructively involved.

When a child bites—"Biting hurts. We use our teeth only to chew food." Never encourage a child to bite back to "show how it feels."

When a child spits—"Your spit belongs in your mouth. If you need to spit, you may spit in the toilet."

When a child uses offensive names—"Do not call Alex 'Stupid.' He is not stupid. He is drawing the way he thinks is best. Alex is doing a good job of drawing. And you are doing a good job of drawing."

When a child has a tantrum—This is no time for words. The child is too upset to listen. Hold the child firmly until he or she calms down. When you hold the child, you are offering protection as well as control. If other children are frightened by the tantrum, take the child to another room with an adult to supervise. Explain to the children, "Katie is having trouble now. She will be all right in a little while."

Redirect Distracting Behavior

Activity does not prevent a child from listening or learning. When a child's active-ness is not interfering with another child's attention, let that child do what his or her energy is requiring at that time. However, there are some general guidelines that can help limit distractions during large group times.

If a child's activity is interfering with another child, signal a teacher or helper to sit beside or behind the active child. The teacher can gently guide arms and legs back into the active child's own space or provide a productive alternate activity the child can do. ("Timmy, if you want to stay here next to John, you must keep your hands in your own lap. Or would you rather come and look at a book?")

Simply state what the child is to do with his or her hands. It is often appropriate to tell the child what will happen if he or she continues to disturb (e.g., be moved to another place).

If the disturbing actions continue, do *exactly* what you said you would do. Your effectiveness depends on your ability to follow through on your promise.

If more than one child is showing signs of restlessness, realize that it's time to do something else (e.g., introduce an instant activity, sing a song, stand and stretch, etc.).

When a child consistently misbehaves during activities, remove the child from the scene of the difficulty. "Marcus, puppets are for playing with, not for tearing. We do not tear toys. I have to put away these puppets." "Jade, you need to come to the game table. I see the Picnic Race game that you like." Keep conversation cheerful.

Help the child handle negative feelings by accepting them. "Jacob, I know you feel angry at Emily for stepping on your dominoes. But you may not hit Emily and Emily may not hit you."

Watch to determine what makes the child want to continue negative behavior. Sometimes misbehavior is simply a bid for attention. Quite often a child would rather be punished (which is one way to get adult attention) than receive no attention.

Avoid repeated threats. There is a difference between a threat ("Wesley, if you do that again, I will . . . ") and explaining consequences ("I cannot let you do that because it might hurt someone."). A threat is a form of a dare that increases tension, while an explanation of consequences (in terms a child can understand) defines limits.

Card Games

Children enjoy surprises, learning, the feeling of achievement and time spent with others while playing games. These games make all this possible because they are designed for a young child's interests and abilities. Rules for some traditional games have been simplified. The game cards picture things young children love and are eager to play with. Each set of game cards can be used with a variety of games

HOW to Prepare the Card Games

☼ Photocopy the pages onto white and/or colored card stock or copier paper (see a game's Preparation instructions for any specifications).

☼ Laminate pages or cover with clear Con-Tact paper.

☼ Cut pages apart along the heavy lines using a paper cutter or scissors.

☼ For a handy collection of games and activities, save each set of prepared materials with a copy of the game and its directions in an envelope, folder or resealable plastic bag.

Charades

Materials: One or more sets of game cards (prepare as instructed on p. 16).

Procedure: Place cards in a facedown stack. Children take turns picking cards from stack and acting out the pictured item for the other children to guess. Play continues as time and interest allow.

For Older Children: For cards more appropriate to an older child's development, choose from these sets—Faces (p. 47), Kitchen Items (p. 71), Instruments (p. 69).

✿ **Group Size:** Two or more players

✿ **Choose from These Sets:** Actions (p.29), Animals at Home (p. 39), Animals in Zoos (p. 41), Animals on Farms (p. 43)

Clap

Materials: Three sets of game cards (prepare as instructed on p. 16).

Procedure: Lead children to play a game similar to Slapjack. Children sit in a circle. Mix the cards and distribute them evenly. Each child places cards facedown in a stack. Before any cards are turned over, declare one set as the Clap set (for example, Leaves). Taking turns, each child takes the top card off his or her stack and lays it faceup on a common pile in the center. Play continues in this manner until a Clap card is laid down. Then each player claps as quickly as possible. The next player takes his or her turn. If a player runs out of cards, he or she may still play game. Play continues until all cards have been played or as time and interest allow.

For Older Children: The first person to clap when a Clap card is laid down picks up the pile in the center and adds it to his or her own stack. Then play resumes. If a player runs out of cards, he or she may get more cards by being the first person to clap when a Clap card is laid down. Play continues as time and interest allow or until one player has all the cards.

✿ **Group Size:** Three to four players

✿ **Choose from These Sets:** Body Parts (p. 45), Faces (p. 47), Flowers (p. 49), Instruments (p. 69), Kitchen Items (p. 71), Leaves (p. 73), Vegetables (p. 91)

Crazy Panda

Materials: Six copies of the panda card (p. 41) and one set of game cards (prepare as instructed on p. 16).

Procedure: Children sit in a circle. Mix the cards and give four cards to each child. Place the remaining cards facedown as a draw pile in the center of the circle. Turn over the top card and lay it faceup beside the draw pile to begin a discard pile. The first player must lay down a card which matches the top card on the discard pile (for example, tractor and tractor silhouette) or a panda card. If neither of these plays can be made, child takes one card from the draw pile and next player takes his or her turn.

If there are no cards left to draw, a child simply says "Pass." Play continues as time and interest allow or until everyone has gotten rid of their cards.

🌼 **Group Size:** Two to four players

🌼 **Choose from These Sets:** Foods and Sources (pp. 51-57), Heads and Tails (pp. 61-67), Mothers and Babies (pp. 75-81), Vehicles and Silhouettes (pp. 93-99)

Does It Have Stripes?

Materials: One set of game cards (prepare as instructed on p. 16).

Procedure: Children sit in a circle. Mix the cards and lay them in a facedown pile in the center. Tell the children which set is being used. One child takes the first card and looks at it without showing it to anyone else. The other children take turns asking questions and guessing what is pictured on the card. ("Does it have legs?" "Is it a cow?") Allow each child one chance to ask a question and make a guess. If no one guesses correctly, child shows card. Play continues as time and interest allow or until each child has had a turn to take a card.

For Younger Children: You may need to look at the drawn cards and prompt the child who is answering questions. Some children asking questions may also need prompting ("Matthew, I wonder if it can swim.").

For Older Children: For cards more appropriate to an older child's development, use the Mothers and Babies set (pp. 75-81).

🌼 **Group Size:** Two to four players

🌼 **Choose from These Sets:** Animals at Home (p. 39), Animals in Zoos (p. 41), Animals on Farms (p. 43), Fruits (p. 59), Instruments (p. 69), Shapes (p. 89)

Find Your Partner

Materials: Two or more copies of one set of game cards (prepare as instructed on p. 16).

Procedure: Give one card to each child, handing out two to three copies of each card. Children holding the same cards form groups by acting out and making the sound of what is pictured on their cards.

For Younger Children: Children show what is on a card instead of acting it out.

For Older Children: For cards more appropriate to an older child's development, choose from these sets— Faces (p. 47), Kitchen Items (p. 71), Instruments (p. 69).

✿ **Group Size:** Two copies of the set for 2 to 16 players; 3 copies for 17 to 24 players

✿ **Choose from These Sets:** Animals at Home (p. 39), Animals on Farms (p. 43)

Hide and Seek

Materials: One set of game cards (prepare as instructed on p. 16).

Procedure: A volunteer picks one card. While other children cover eyes, volunteer hides card in a visible place in the room. At your signal, children uncover eyes and look for the card. Whoever finds it chooses another card and hides it. If a child has already had a turn, choose a child who has not had a turn to hide a card. Play continues as time and interest allow or until every child has had a turn.

✿ **Group Size:** Two to eight players

✿ **Choose from These Sets:** Alphabet (pp. 31-37), Animals on Farms (p. 43), Fruits (p. 59), Kitchen Items (p. 71), Numbers (pp. 83-87)

Lonely Dandelion

Materials: The dandelion card (p. 49) and two copies of two sets of game cards (prepare as instructed on p. 16).

Procedure: Children sit in a circle. Lead the children to play a game similar to Old Maid. Mix the cards and distribute to the children (some children may have one more card than other players). Children match any pairs they are holding and lay them faceup in the middle of the circle.

After pairs are laid down, the first player holds out his or her cards facedown to the player on his or her left, who chooses one card. If that card makes a pair with any cards in the child's hand, the pair is laid faceup in the center. If not, the player keeps the card. Play continues around the circle until every pair has been laid down, and the dandelion card is the only one left.

For Older Children: For cards more appropriate to an older child's development, choose one of these sets—Foods and Sources (pp. 51-57), Heads and Tails (pp. 61-67), Mothers and Babies (pp. 75-81), Vehicles and Silhouettes (pp. 93-99). (Since these cards come in pairs, it is not necessary to make copies.)

✿ **Group Size:** Two to four players

✿ **Choose from These Sets:** Actions (p. 29), Animals in Zoos (p. 41), Fruits (p. 59), Kitchen Items (p. 71), Shapes (p. 89), Weather (p. 101)

Make a Pair

Materials: Two copies of one set of game cards (prepare as instructed on p. 16).

Procedure: Children sit in a circle. Line up one set of cards faceup, and make a facedown pile of the other set. Players take turns taking one facedown card from the pile and laying it on its match. Lead children to name the card when laying it down.

For Younger Children: Children place cards without naming them.

For Older Children: For cards more appropriate to an older child's development, choose from these sets—Foods and Sources (pp. 51-57), Heads and Tails (pp. 61-67), Mothers and Babies (pp. 75-81), Vehicles and Silhouettes (pp. 93-99). (Optional: Child acts out the card after laying it down.)

✿ **Group Size:** One to four players

✿ **Choose from These Sets:** Alphabet (pp. 31-37), Numbers (pp. 83-87)

Match!

Materials: Five copies of one set of game cards (prepare as instructed on p. 16).

Procedure: Children sit in a circle. Mix and hand out all cards, one facedown stack in front of each child. One child turns over the top card from his or her stack and lays it faceup in the center of the circle. The next child turns over his or her top card and lays it on top of the faceup card. If the two cards are the same, that player picks up the stack of faceup cards. If they are not identical, the next child turns a card over and lays it on the other faceup cards. Play continues as time and interest allow or until one person has all the cards.

For Older Children: If the two cards are the same, the first child to call out "Match!" picks up the stack. (Optional: If a player incorrectly calls "Match!" that player places two cards on the center stack.)

✿ **Group size:** Two to four players

✿ **Choose from These Sets:** Animals on Farms (p. 43), Fruits (p. 59), Instruments (p. 69), Kitchen Items (p. 71), Leaves (p. 73), Vegetables (p. 91), Weather (p. 101)

Memory Match

Materials: Two copies of one or two sets of cards (prepare as instructed on p. 16).

Procedure: Mix the cards and place them facedown in rows. Children take turns turning over two cards in search of a pair. If cards match, child takes the pair and turns over two more. If cards do not match, child turns them facedown again and the next child takes a turn. Play continues as time and interest allow or until all cards have been matched.

Variation: Use three copies of a set instead of one or two. Children turn over three cards at a time, looking for three cards that match.

For Younger Children: Children turn over only one card at a time. Each card that has been turned over remains faceup.

For Older Children: For cards more appropriate to an older child's development, choose from these sets—Foods and Sources (pp. 51-57), Heads and Tails (pp. 61-67), Mothers and Babies (pp. 75-81), Vehicles and Silhouettes (pp. 93-99). (Note: Do not make copies because these sets already include pairs.)

✿ **Group Size:** Two to four players

✿ **Choose from These Sets:** Animals at Home (p. 39), Body Parts (p.45), Faces (p. 47), Flowers (p. 49), Shapes (p. 89), Vegetables (p. 91), Weather (p. 101)

Numbers Teams

Materials: One set of Numbers cards (prepare as instructed on p. 16), 30 to 40 small classroom or household items (crayons, small blocks, drinking straws, etc.).

Procedure: Group children into teams of two or three. Place classroom or household items in a central location. Give each team a number card. Each team collects the same number of items as is printed on their card. When each team is done, a member of each team returns items to central location. Repeat activity as time and interest allow.

For Older Children: Children work individually rather than in teams.

❀ **Group Size:** Four to nine players

❀ **Choose This Set:** Numbers (pp. 83-87)

Pick a Card!

Materials: Two copies of either the Alphabet or Numbers set (prepare as instructed on p. 16).

Procedure: Lead the children to play a game like Go Fish. Children sit in a circle. Mix the cards and hand out five cards to each child. Place the leftover cards facedown in a draw pile in the center of the circle. The first child asks any other player for a card which would match one in his or her hand. If the other player has that card, that player gives it to the asker. When the asker gets a pair, he or she lays it down faceup and asks any other player for another card. If the other player does not have the card asked for, he or she responds "Pick a card." Then the asker draws a card from the pile. The player to the child's left takes a turn. Play continues as time and interest allow or until all pairs have been laid down.

For Younger Children: Hand out only three cards per child (three cards are easier for a young child to hold).

❀ **Group Size:** Two to four players

❀ **Choose from These Sets:** Alphabet (pp. 31-37), Numbers (pp. 83-87)

Seek and You Will Find

Materials: One or more sets of game cards (prepare as instructed on p. 16).

Procedure: Before children arrive or while eyes are covered, hide one card for each child. At your signal, children look for cards, with each child bringing one card back to you. Play continues until all cards have been found or as time and interest allow.

For Older Children: For cards more appropriate to an older child's development, choose either the Alphabet (pp. 31-37) or Numbers set (pp. 83-87). As the children find cards, they place them in order.

 **Group Size:** One set for 2 to 8 players; 2 sets for 9 to 16 players

❀ **Choose from These Sets:** Animals on Farms (p. 43), Body Parts (p. 45), Faces (p.47), Flowers (p. 49), Leaves (p. 73), Vegetables (p. 91)

Shape Search

Materials: One set of Shape cards (prepare as instructed on p. 16).

Procedure: Give a card to each child, asking each child to touch his or her card to something in the room with the same shape. Collect cards and redistribute, having children find other items if possible. Play continues as time and interest allow.

❀ **Group Size:** One to eight players

❀ **Choose This Set:** Shapes (p. 89)

What Color Are You Eating?

Materials: One set of Fruits cards and one set of Vegetables cards (prepare as instructed on p. 16); crayons, blocks or other items in red, orange, yellow, brown, green and purple.

Procedure: Place the colored items in a row. Lay the cards facedown in a draw pile. Each child takes a turn to pick the top card and lay it down in front of the item of matching color. Play continues as time and interest allow or until all cards have been used.

✿ **Group Size:** One to four players

✿ **Choose These Sets:** Fruits (p. 59), Vegetables (p. 91)

Where Do I Live?

Materials: One or more sets of Animal cards (prepare as instructed on p. 16).

Procedure: Children sit in a circle. Mix the cards and lay them facedown in one pile in the center of the circle. Children take turns to pick the top card, identify the pictured animal and tell where the animal lives (in a zoo, in a barn, in a house, etc.). Play continues around the circle of children until all cards have been used.

Variation: Player makes a sound like or acts like the animal on the card.

For Younger Children: Set up a zoo area, a farm area and a house area (use toy buildings or magazine pictures as scenes). When child turns over a card, he or she puts the card in the appropriate area.

✿ **Group Size:** One to four players

✿ **Choose from These sets:** Animals at Home (p. 39), Animals in Zoos (p. 41), Animals on Farms (p. 43), Mothers and Babies (pp. 75-81)

Alphabet Treasure Hunt

Materials: One set of Alphabet cards, except *Q, X* and *Z* (prepare as instructed on p. 16).

Procedure: Children form groups of two or three. Give each group a card. Each group finds a classroom item that begins with the letter on its card and touches the card to it. Play continues as time and interest allow or until all cards have been used.

Variation: Children work individually rather than in groups.

❁ **Group Size:** One to nine players

❁ **Choose This Set:** Alphabet (pp. 31-37)

Giveaway

Materials: One set of Alphabet cards and one set of Numbers cards (prepare as instructed on p. 16).

Procedure: Children sit in a circle. Mix cards and distribute five to each child. The first player lays any card faceup in the center of the circle. The next child lays a card from the matching set on top of the card already faceup. Play continues around the circle. When a player cannot lay down a card from the matching set, he or she picks up the entire stack of cards and adds it to his or her own cards. Then that player lays down any card. Play continues as time and interest allow or until one child has played his or her last card.

Variation: Distribute seven or eight cards to each child.

❁ **Group Size:** Three to four players

❁ **Choose These Sets:** Alphabet (pp. 31-37), Numbers (pp. 83-87)

Please and Thank You

Materials: One set of game cards (prepare as instructed on p. 16).

Procedure: Lead the children to play a game similar to Go Fish but in which politeness must be practiced. Children sit in a circle. Mix the cards and hand them all out (some children may have one more card than other players). The first child asks any other player for a card which matches a card in the asker's hand. If the other player has that card, that player gives it to the asker. The asker must say "Please" when asking for a card and "Thank you" when receiving a card. If a card is handed over without "Please" and "Thank you" being said, the card must be given back. When the asker gets a pair, he or she lays it down faceup and asks any other player for another card. If the other player does not have the card asked for, the child's turn is over. Play continues around the circle as time and interest allow or until all pairs have been laid down.

✿ **Group Size:** Two to four players

✿ **Choose from These Sets:** Foods and Sources (pp. 51-57), Heads and Tails (pp. 61-67), Mothers and Babies (pp. 75-81), Vehicles and Silhouettes (pp. 93-99)

Sound Sort

Materials: One set of game cards plus the Alphabet cards (prepare as instructed on p. 16).

Procedure: Mix the Alphabet cards and distribute them to children. Children place the cards faceup on floor or table in order from *A* to *Z*. Then hand out the second set of game cards to children. Children take turns saying the first letter of each item pictured and placing the card by its corresponding letter. Match the pictures with the first letter for each picture. Play continues as time and interest allow or until the last card has been played.

✿ **Group Size:** One to four players

✿ **Choose from These Sets:** Animals at Home (p. 39), Fruits (p. 59), Instruments (p. 69), Kitchen Items (p. 71), Leaves (p. 73), Vegetables (p. 91), Weather (p. 101)

Spoons

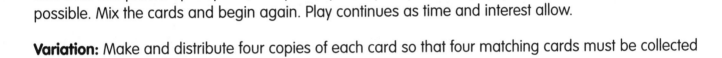

Materials: Three copies of one set of game cards (prepare as instructed on p. 16), one plastic spoon for each player.

Procedure: Remove enough cards so that there are exactly three matching cards per player. Children sit in a circle. Mix the cards and give three to each child. Children hold their cards so that any matching cards are together. Evenly space out the spoons in the center of the circle. At your signal, each child lays down a nonmatching card by the child on his or her left and then picks up the card just laid down by the child to his or her right. Repeat this procedure until one child has three of the same card. That child picks up a spoon. When one child has picked up a spoon, every child picks up a spoon as quickly as possible. Mix the cards and begin again. Play continues as time and interest allow.

Variation: Make and distribute four copies of each card so that four matching cards must be collected before a spoon is picked up.

✿ **Group Size:** Three to six players

✿ **Choose from These Sets:** Actions (p. 29), Animals on Farms (p. 43), Body Parts (p. 45), Faces (p. 47), Flowers (p. 49), Shapes (p. 89)

Zigzag

Materials: One set of game cards (prepare as instructed on p. 16).

Procedure: Children sit in a circle. Mix cards and give them all out (some children may have one more card than other players). Choose one child who has an extra card to play first. The first player says "Zig" and lays down any card in the center of the circle. Whoever has the card which corresponds to the one laid down (corn kernels and ear of corn, for example) says "Zag" and lays down the corresponding card on the first card. Play continues around the circle: the child to the left of the one who first said "Zig" lays down any card and says "Zig," and another child follows with "Zag" and a corresponding card. Play continues as time and interest allow or until all cards have been played.

Variation: Use other pairs of words for children to say ("Hot" and "Cold," "Up" and "Down," "Hippety" and "Hop" or even "Hinkety" and "Pinkety").

✿ **Group Size:** Three to four players

✿ **Choose from These Sets:** Foods and Sources (pp. 51-57), Heads and Tails (pp. 61-67), Mothers and Babies (pp. 75-81), Vehicles and Silhouettes (pp. 93-99)

Actions

Actions

Actions

Actions

Actions

Actions

Actions

Actions

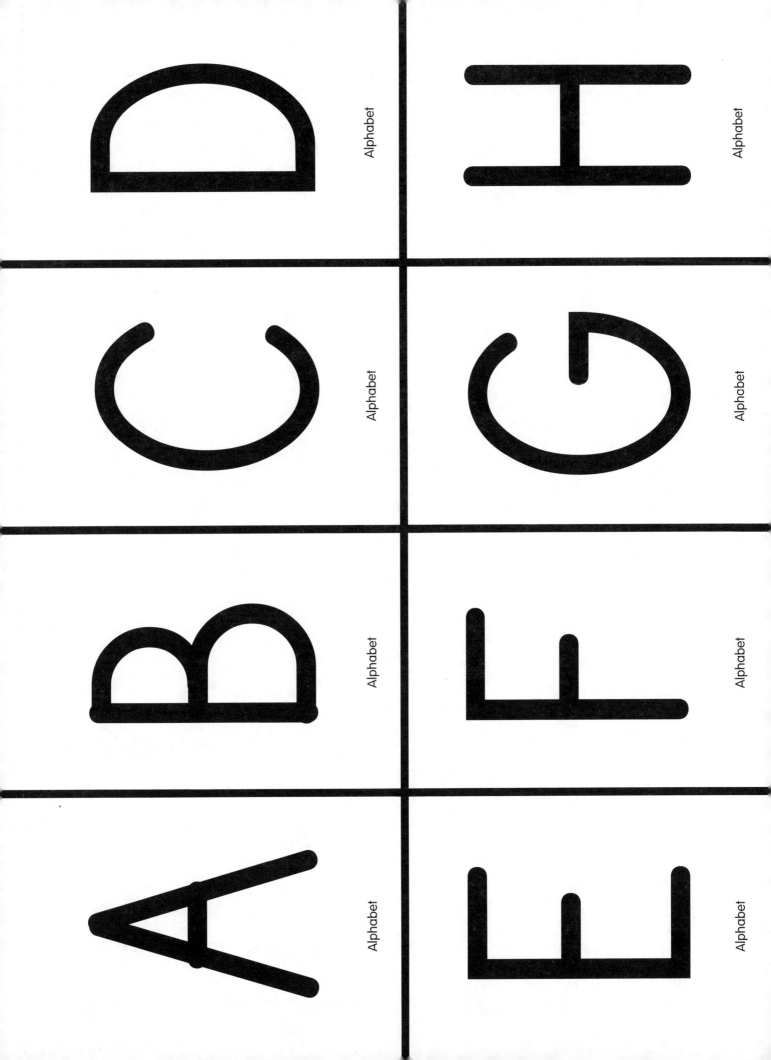

D

Alphabet

H

Alphabet

C

Alphabet

G

Alphabet

B

Alphabet

F

Alphabet

A

Alphabet

E

Alphabet

L

Alphabet

P

Alphabet

K

Alphabet

O

Alphabet

J

Alphabet

N

Alphabet

I

Alphabet

M

Alphabet

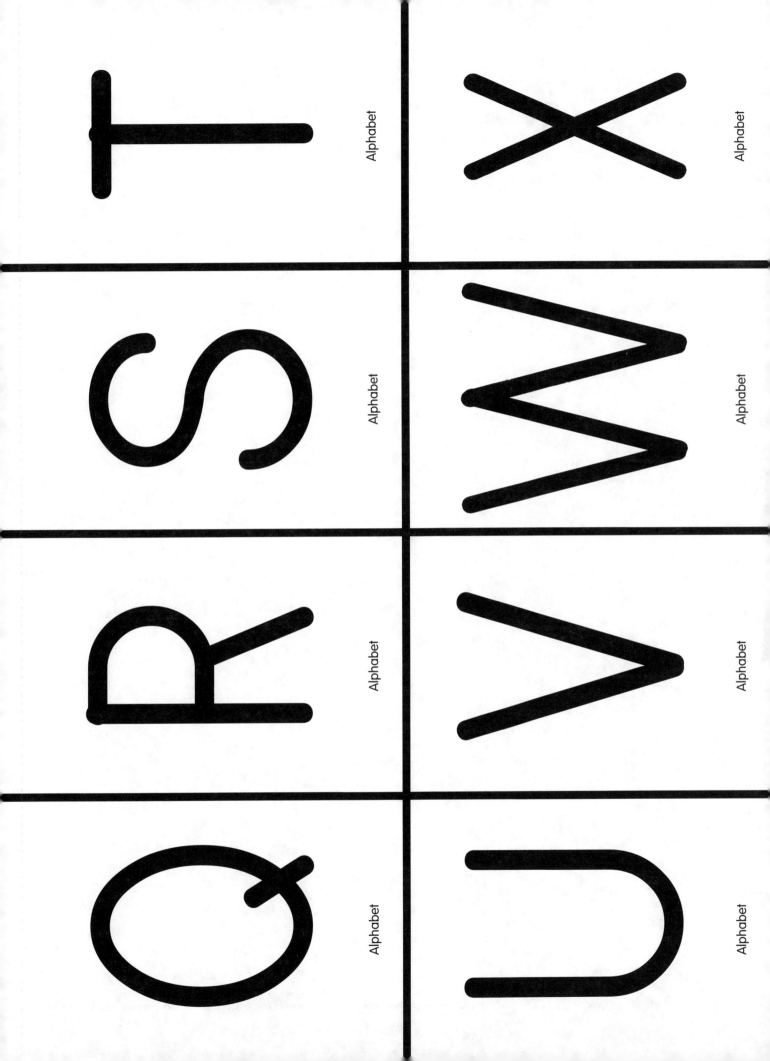

T

Alphabet

X

Alphabet

S

Alphabet

W

Alphabet

R

Alphabet

V

Alphabet

Q

Alphabet

U

Alphabet

Z

Alphabet

Y

Alphabet

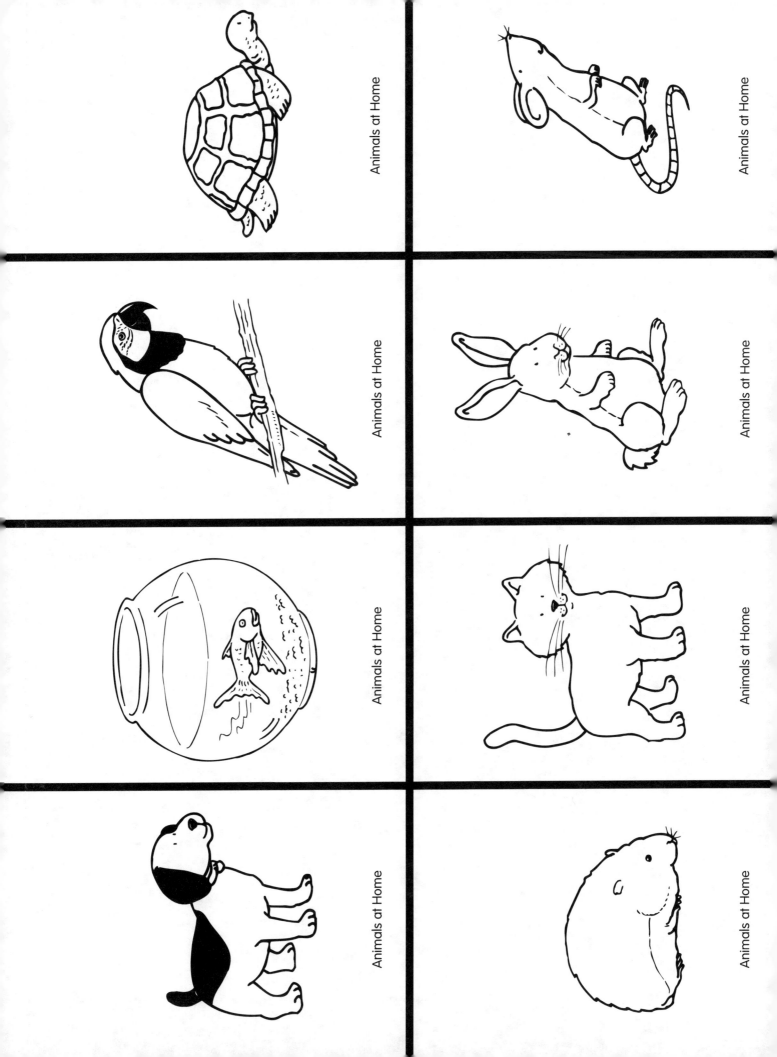

Animals at Home

Animals at Home

Animals at Home

Animals at Home

Animals at Home

Animals at Home

Animals at Home

Animals at Home

Animals in Zoos

Animals in Zoos

Animals in Zoos

Animals in Zoos

Animals in Zoos

Animals in Zoos

Animals in Zoos

Animals in Zoos

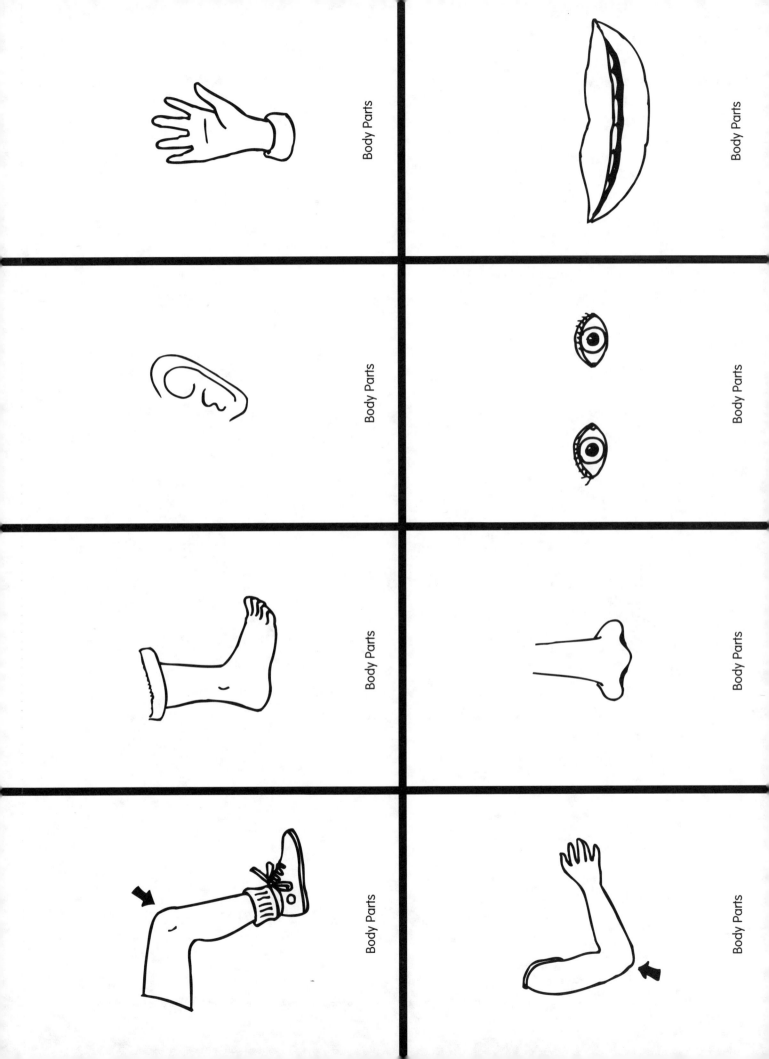

Body Parts

Body Parts

Body Parts

Body Parts

Body Parts

Body Parts

Body Parts

Body Parts

Faces

Faces

Faces

Faces

Faces

Faces

Flowers

Flowers

Flowers

Flowers

Flowers

Flowers

Flowers

Flowers

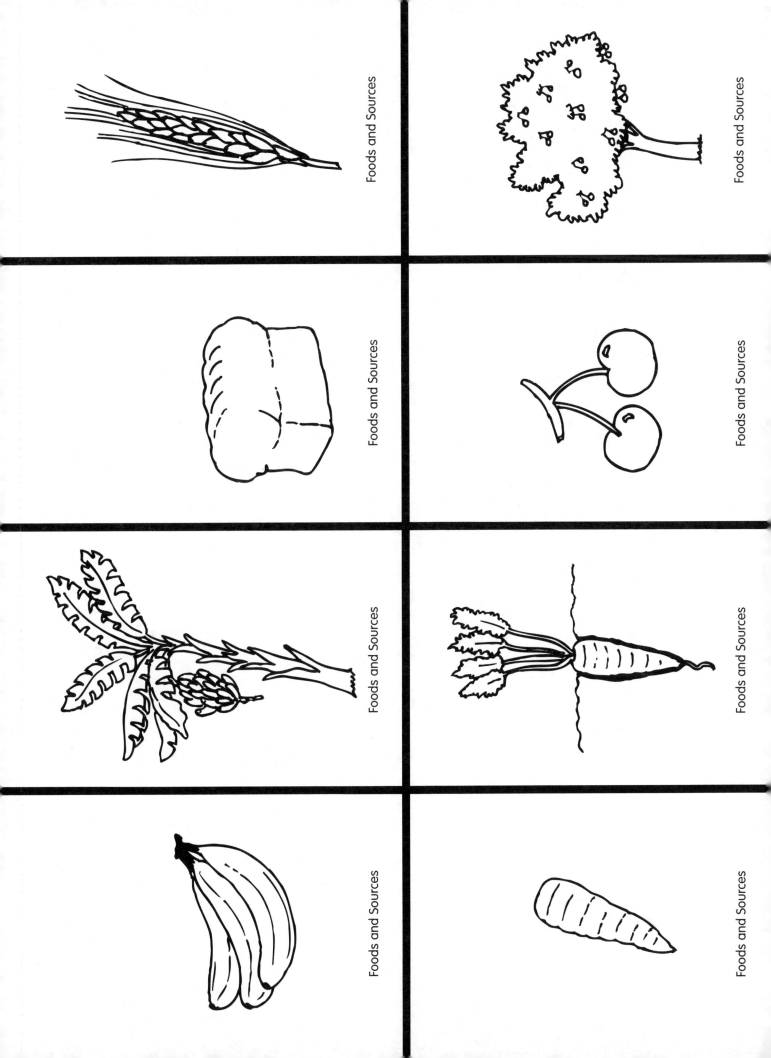

Foods and Sources

Foods and Sources

Foods and Sources

Foods and Sources

Foods and Sources

Foods and Sources

Foods and Sources

Foods and Sources

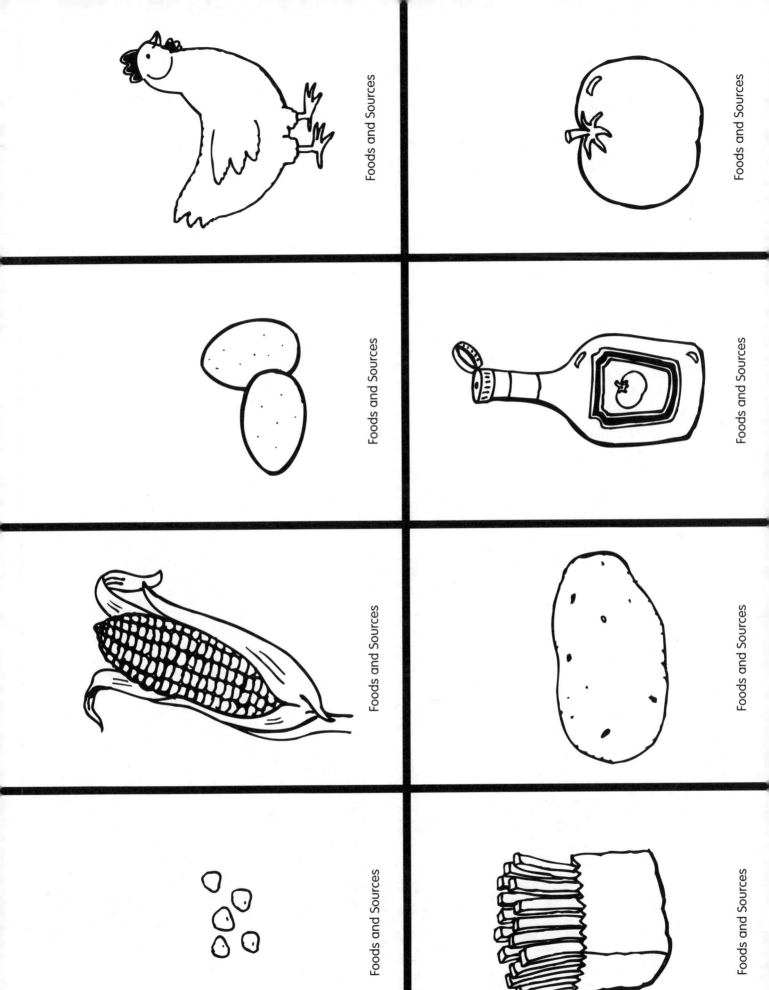

Foods and Sources

Foods and Sources

Foods and Sources

Foods and Sources

Foods and Sources

Foods and Sources

Foods and Sources

Foods and Sources

Foods and Sources

Foods and Sources

Foods and Sources

Foods and Sources

Foods and Sources

Foods and Sources

Foods and Sources

Foods and Sources

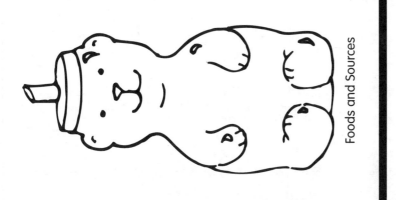

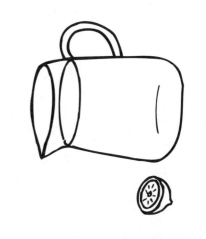

Fruits

Fruits

Fruits

Fruits

Fruits

Fruits

Fruits

Fruits

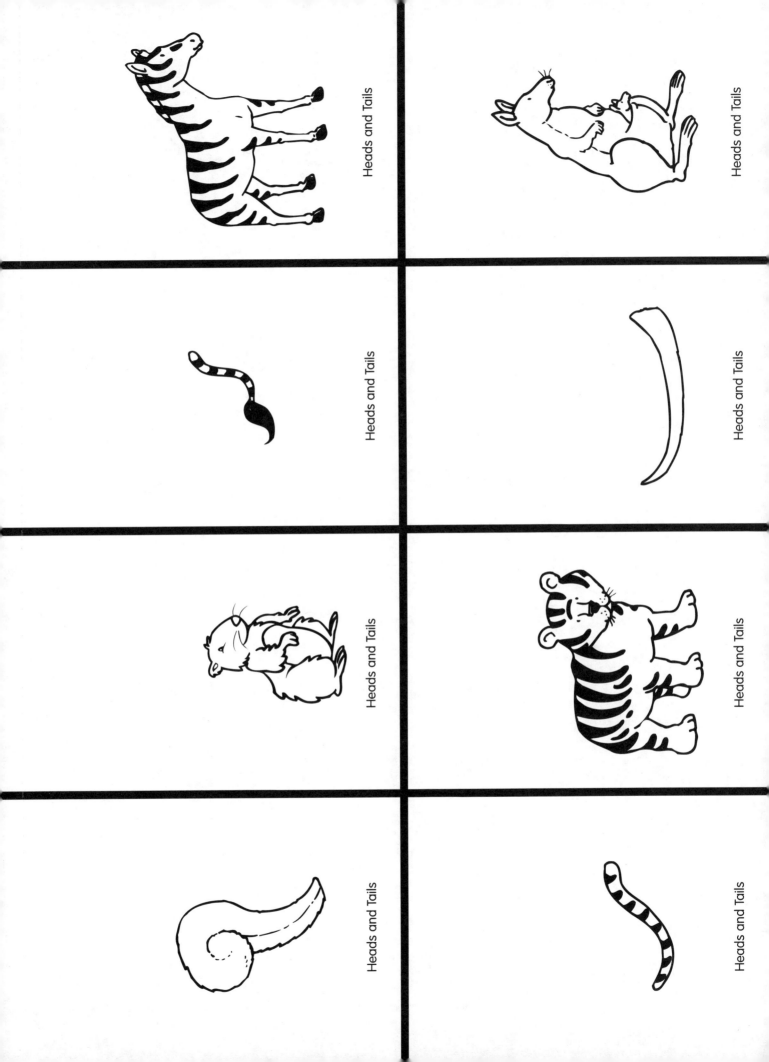

Heads and Tails

Heads and Tails

Heads and Tails

Heads and Tails

Heads and Tails

Heads and Tails

Heads and Tails

Heads and Tails

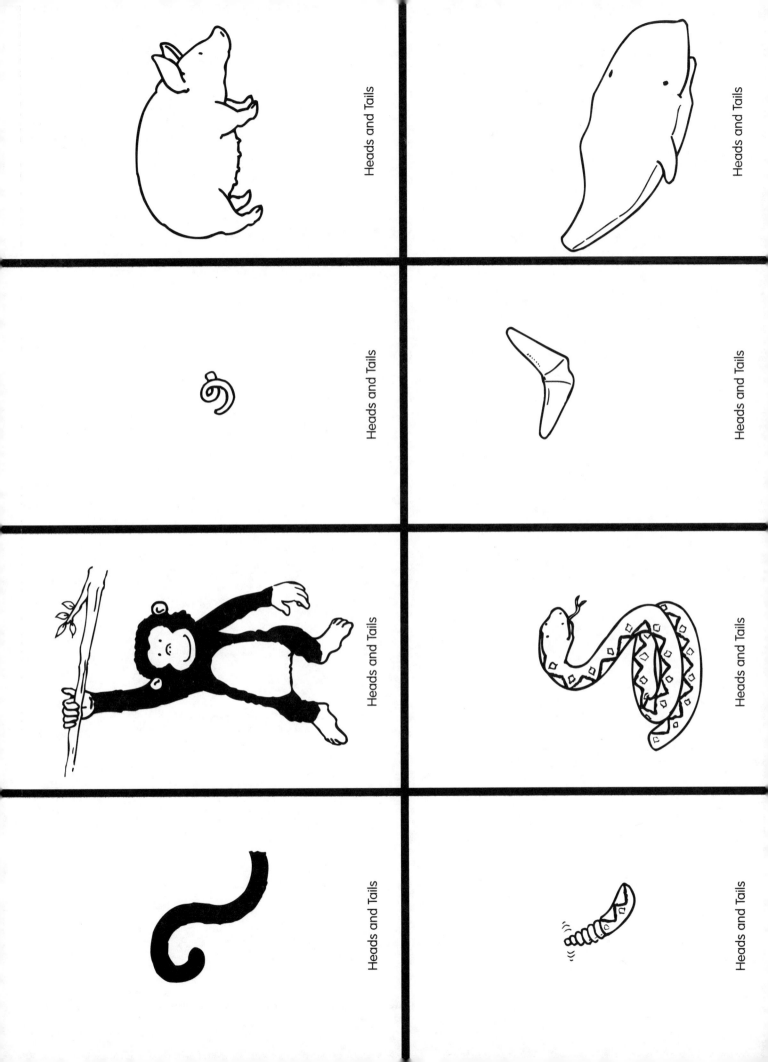

Heads and Tails

Heads and Tails

Heads and Tails

Heads and Tails

Heads and Tails

Heads and Tails

Heads and Tails

Heads and Tails

Heads and Tails

Heads and Tails

Heads and Tails

Heads and Tails

Heads and Tails

Heads and Tails

Heads and Tails

Heads and Tails

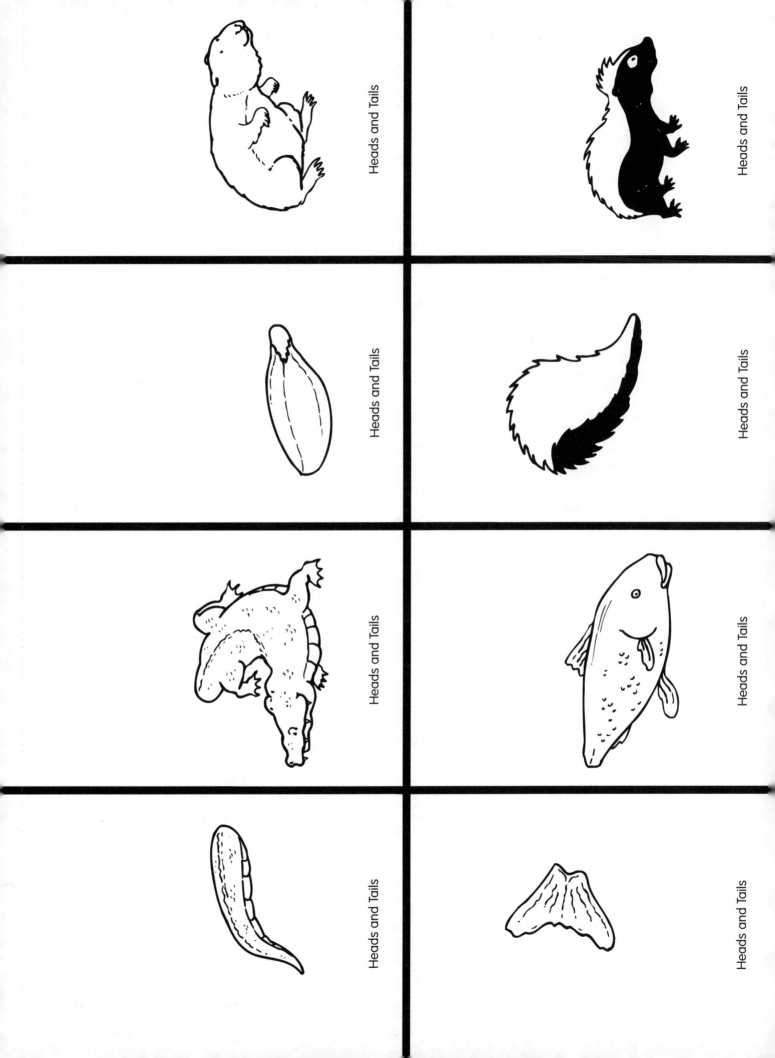

Heads and Tails

Heads and Tails

Heads and Tails

Heads and Tails

Heads and Tails

Heads and Tails

Heads and Tails

Heads and Tails

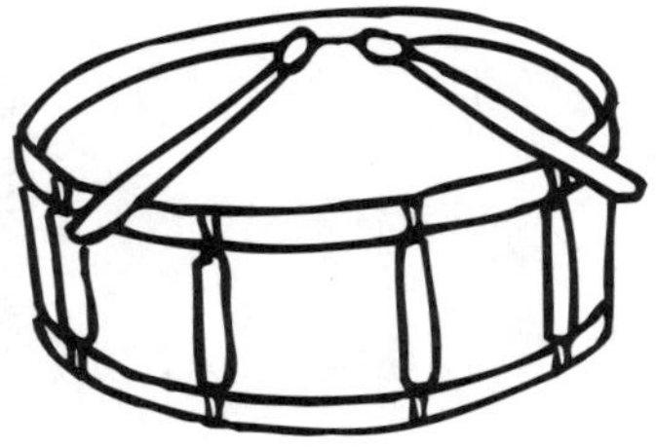

Instruments

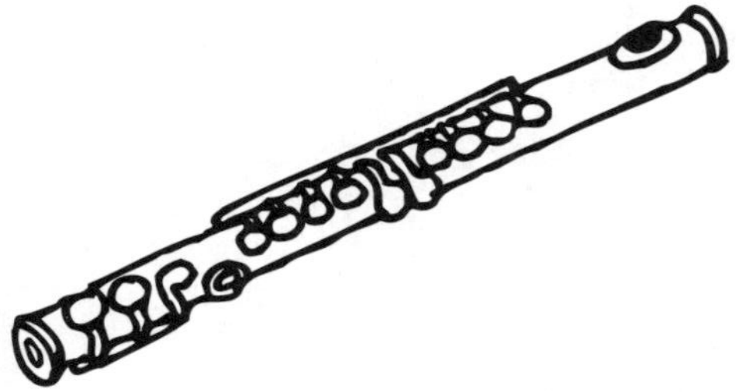

Instruments

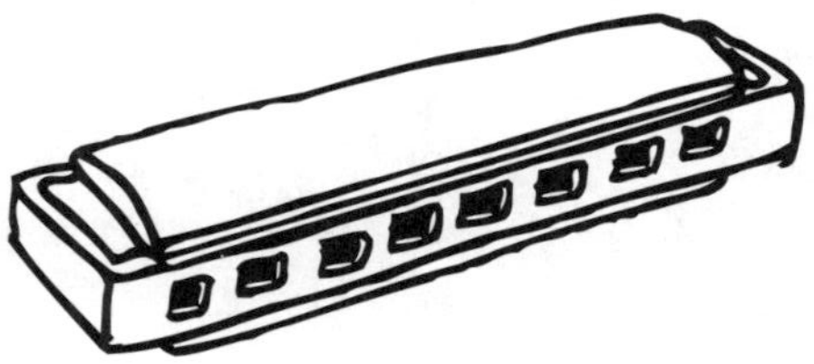

Instruments

Instruments

Instruments

Instruments

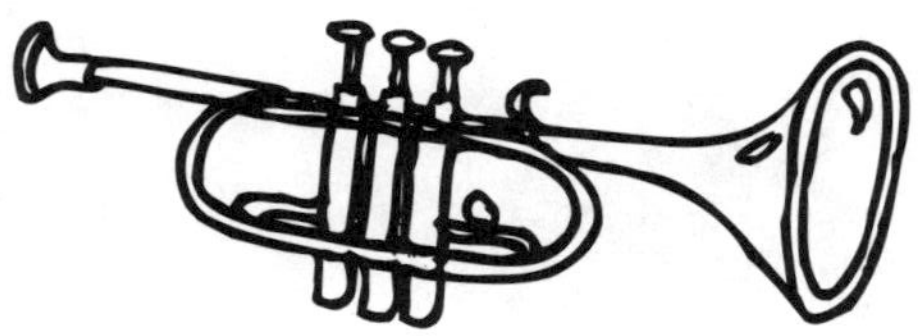

Instruments

Instruments

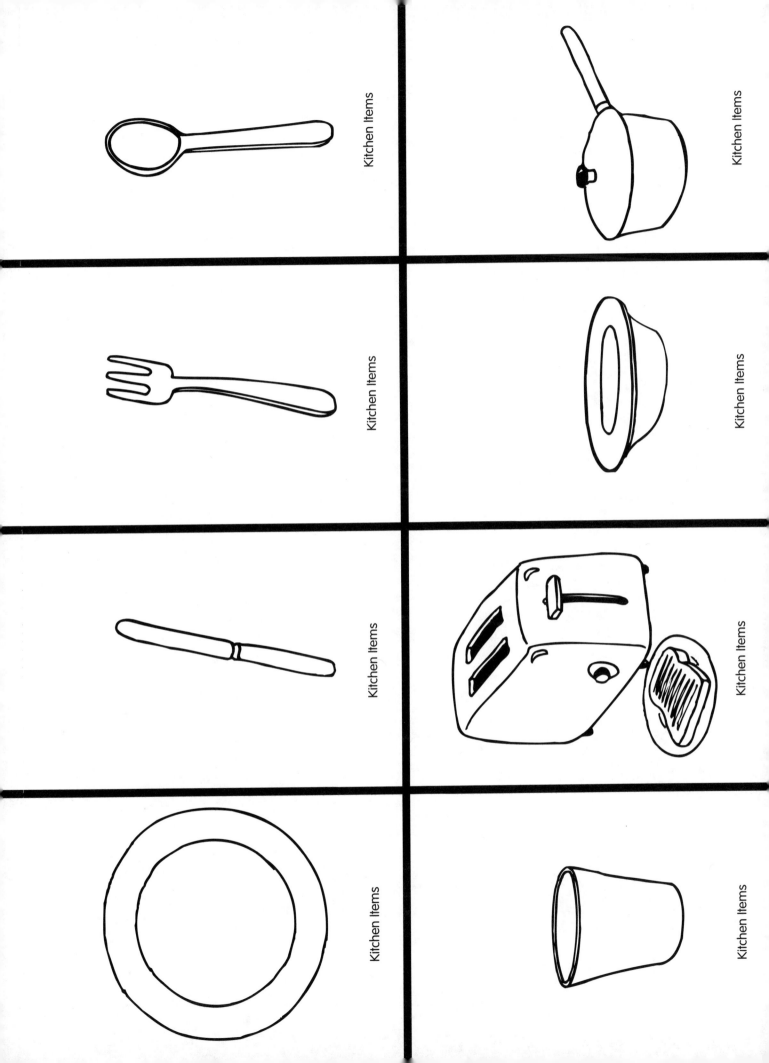

Kitchen Items

Kitchen Items

Kitchen Items

Kitchen Items

Kitchen Items

Kitchen Items

Kitchen Items

Kitchen Items

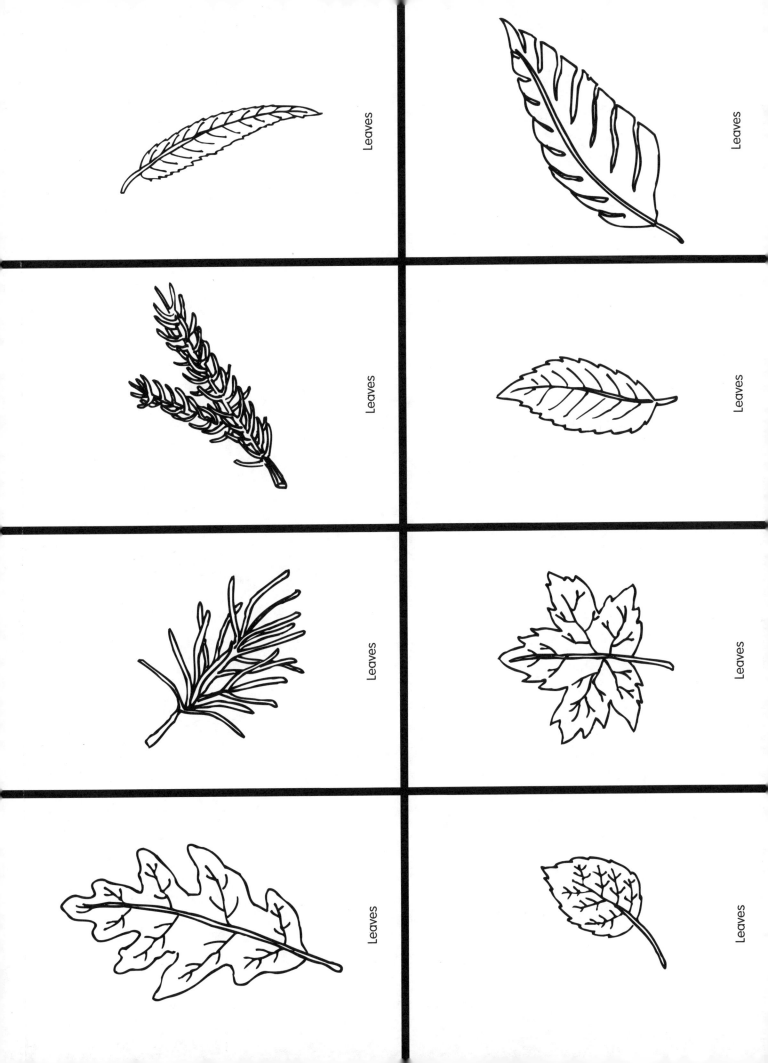

Leaves

Leaves

Leaves

Leaves

Leaves

Leaves

Leaves

Leaves

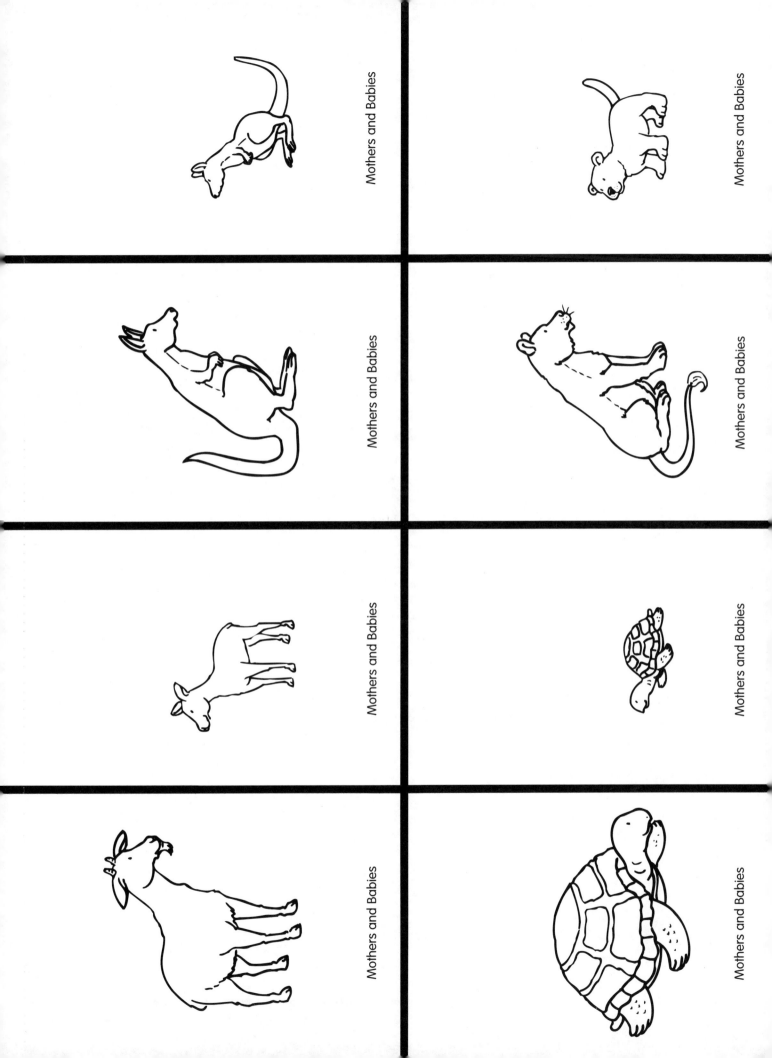

Mothers and Babies

Mothers and Babies

Mothers and Babies

Mothers and Babies

Mothers and Babies

Mothers and Babies

Mothers and Babies

Mothers and Babies

Mothers and Babies

Mothers and Babies

Mothers and Babies

Mothers and Babies

Mothers and Babies

Mothers and Babies

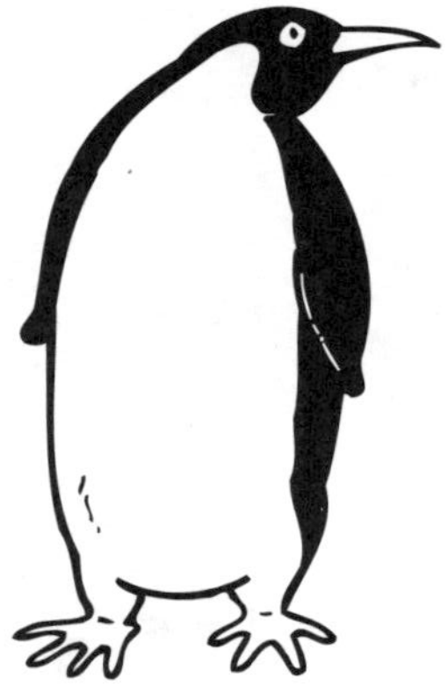

Mothers and Babies

Mothers and Babies

Mothers and Babies

Mothers and Babies

Mothers and Babies

Mothers and Babies

Mothers and Babies

Mothers and Babies

Mothers and Babies

Mothers and Babies

Mothers and Babies

Mothers and Babies

Mothers and Babies

Mothers and Babies

Mothers and Babies

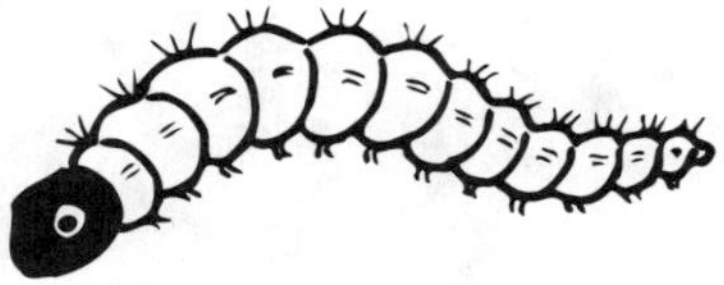

Mothers and Babies

Mothers and Babies

Mothers and Babies

3

7

2

6

1

5

0

4

11

Numbers

15

Numbers

10

Numbers

14

Numbers

9

Numbers

13

Numbers

8

Numbers

12

Numbers

19

Numbers

18

Numbers

17

Numbers

16

Numbers

20

Numbers

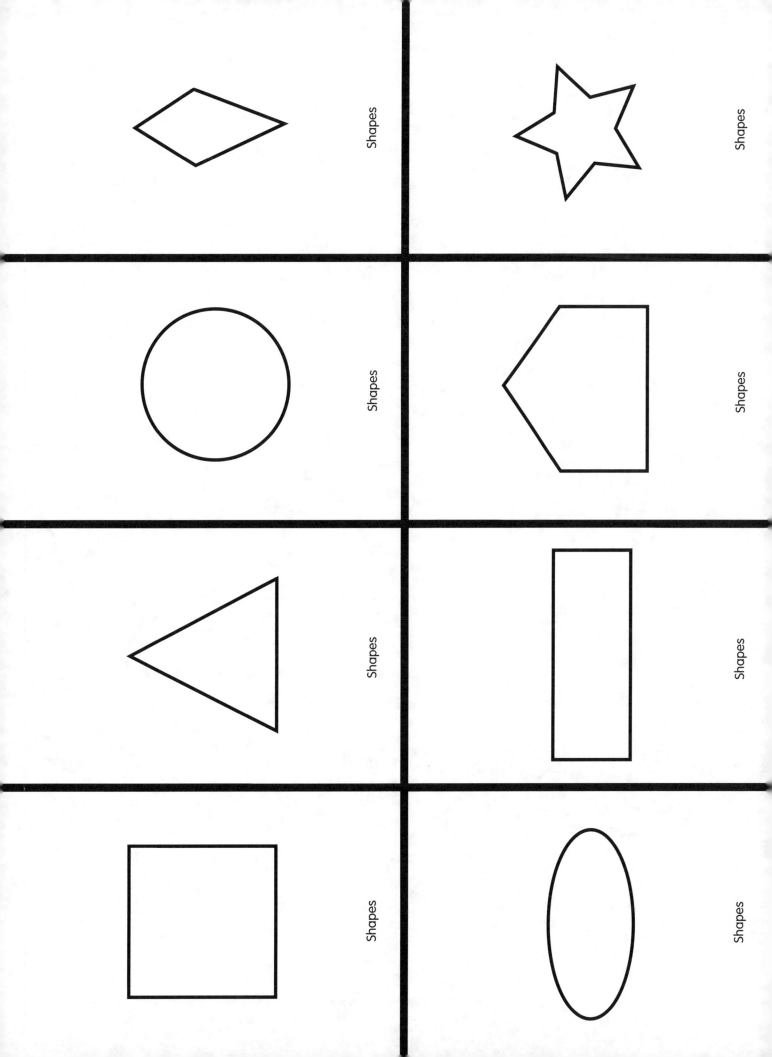

Shapes

Shapes

Shapes

Shapes

Shapes

Shapes

Shapes

Shapes

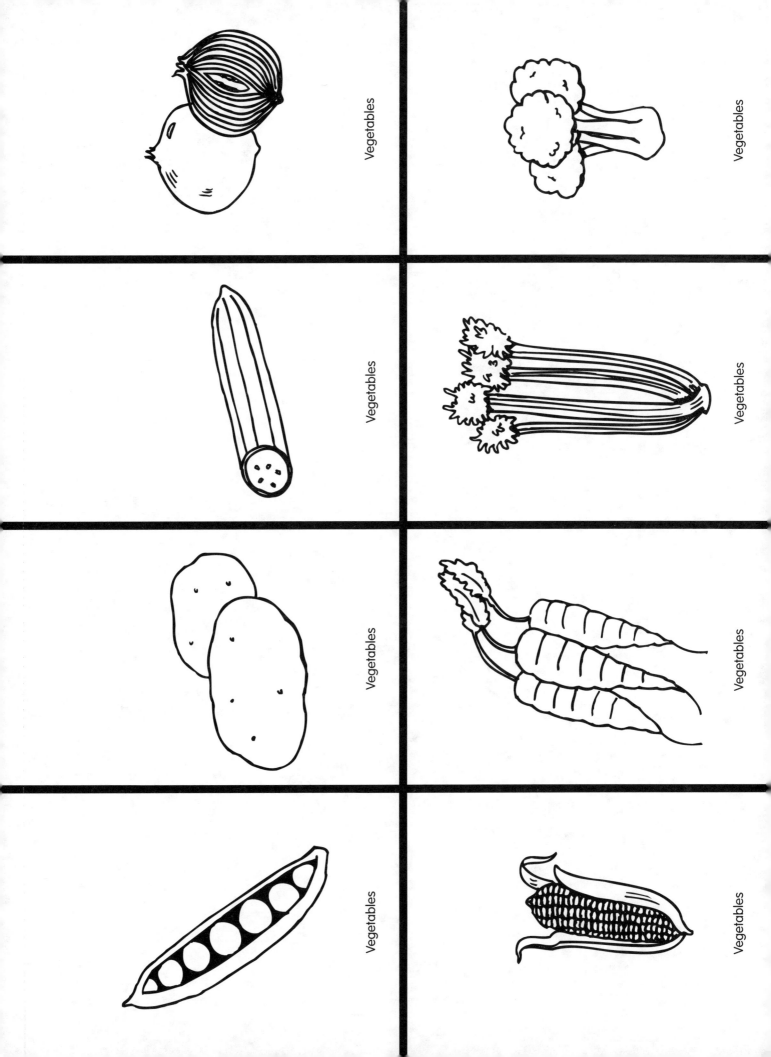

Vegetables

Vegetables

Vegetables

Vegetables

Vegetables

Vegetables

Vegetables

Vegetables

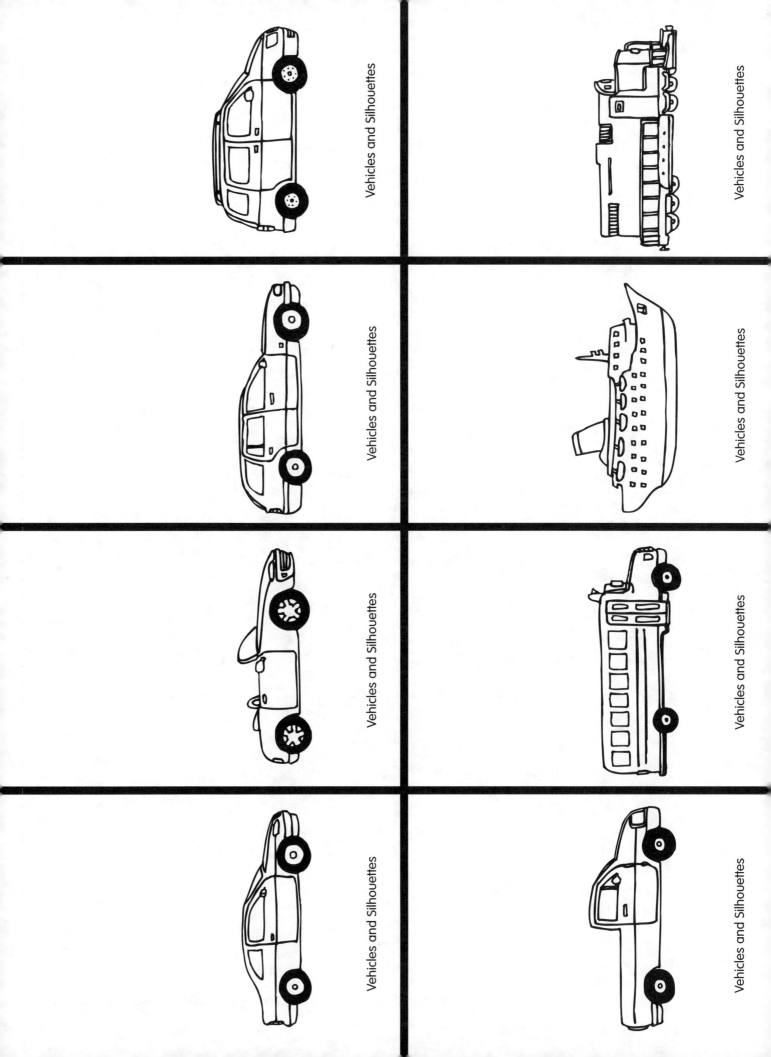

Vehicles and Silhouettes

Vehicles and Silhouettes

Vehicles and Silhouettes

Vehicles and Silhouettes

Vehicles and Silhouettes

Vehicles and Silhouettes

Vehicles and Silhouettes

Vehicles and Silhouettes

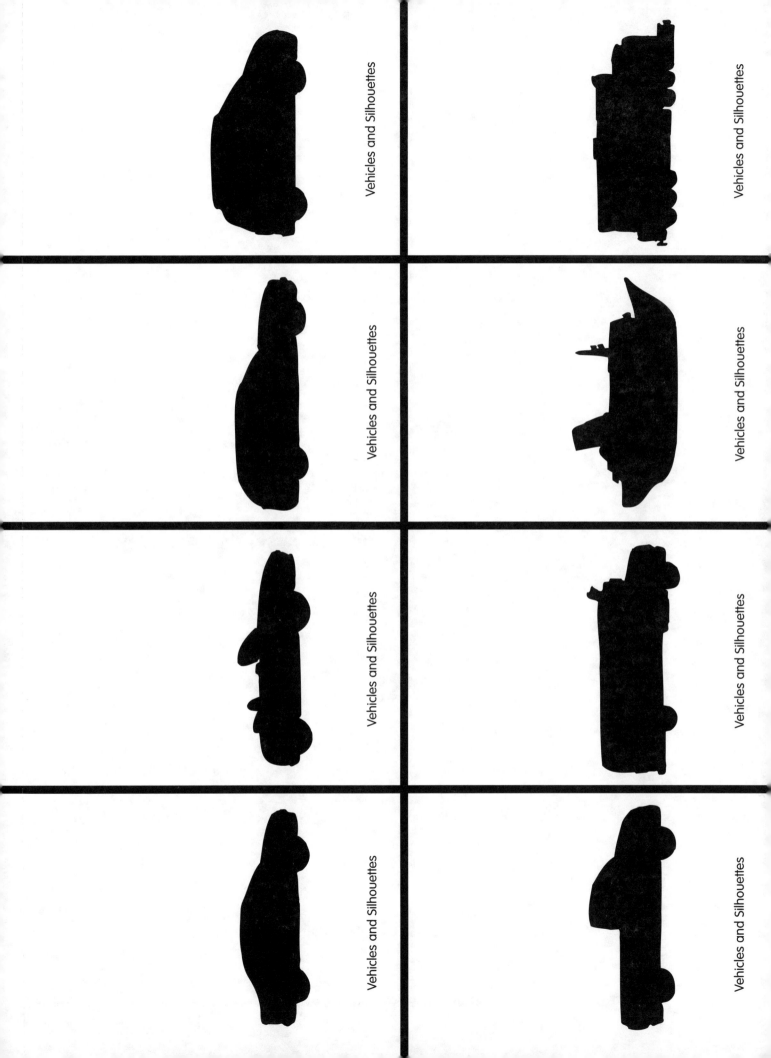

Vehicles and Silhouettes

Vehicles and Silhouettes

Vehicles and Silhouettes

Vehicles and Silhouettes

Vehicles and Silhouettes

Vehicles and Silhouettes

Vehicles and Silhouettes

Vehicles and Silhouettes

Vehicles and Silhouettes

Vehicles and Silhouettes

Vehicles and Silhouettes

Vehicles and Silhouettes

Vehicles and Silhouettes

Vehicles and Silhouettes

Vehicles and Silhouettes

Vehicles and Silhouettes

Weather

Weather

Weather

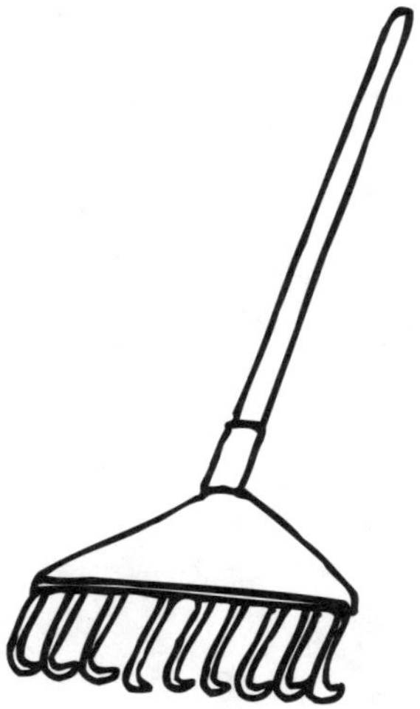

Weather

Weather

Weather

Weather

Weather

Board Games

Children will experience a tremendous variety of play and activity with these delightful new games. Sometimes young children will be hopping, sometimes building, sometimes matching—and always having fun! All the resources for these games are right here in the book.

HOW to Prepare the Board Games and Cards

☼ Photocopy the pages onto white and/or colored card stock or copier paper (see a game's Preparation instructions for any specifications).

☼ Laminate pages or cover with clear Con-Tact paper.

☼ Cut pages apart along the heavy lines using a paper cutter or scissors.

☼ For a handy collection of games and activities, save each set of prepared materials with a copy of the game and its directions in an envelope, folder or resealable plastic bag.

Animal Race

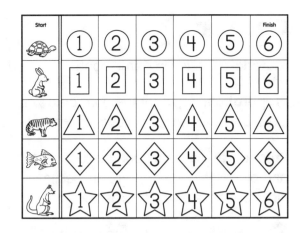

Materials: Animal Race game board and cards (pp. 111-113).

Preparation: Make one copy of game board and three copies of cards (prepare as instructed on p. 104). To make game markers, cut off column of animals from right edge of board.

Procedure: Mix cards and place them facedown in a pile near the game board. Give each child an animal game marker. Each child sets his or her game marker on the matching animal on the game board. First player draws the top card from the pile and names the shape aloud. Whichever player whose animal game marker has that shape by its picture, moves ahead one space. If a child draws the shape for his or her own animal game marker, then he or she advances two spaces. Next child draws a card. Play continues as time and interest allow or until all players have reached the finish column.

For Younger Children: Rather than using cards to move markers forward, use a simple spinner. To make the spinner, draw a circle with a line dividing it in half. Write a "1" in one half and a "2" in the other. Place the tip of a pen or pencil in the center of the circle and spin a paper clip around the tip as the spinner's pointer. The player moves the game marker one or two spaces according to whether the paper clip points to the "1" or "2" section.

✿ **Group Size:** Three to six players

✿ **Goal:** Get to the finish line first. Players move forward whenever their animal's shape card is drawn.

Animals Everywhere

Materials: Animals Everywhere game board and cards (pp. 115-117).

Preparation: Copy game board and cards (prepare as instructed on p. 104).

Procedure: Mix cards and place them facedown in a draw pile. First player takes the top card from the pile and names the animal aloud. Child places card on section of game board that shows where animal might live. Play continues until all animals have been placed or time is called. (Note: Some animals fit multiple environments [butterfly or ant], and children might imagine a situation for their choice. "Matthew, why do you have the dog underground?" "Yes, sometimes a dog will dig a hole to bury a bone.")

✿ **Group Size:** One to six players

✿ **Goal:** Sort animals by where they live.

Clean Up

Materials: Clean Up game board and cards (pp. 119-121).

Preparation: Copy game board onto white card stock or copier paper; copy cards onto colored card stock or copier paper (follow remaining preparation instructions on p. 104).

Procedure: Mix cards and place them facedown in a draw pile. First player takes top card from pile and places it in the appropriate section on the game board to show how room has been cleaned up. Play continues until all cards have been placed on the game board.

🌸 **Group Size:** One to three players

🌸 **Goal:** Show ways of cleaning up a messy room by covering the messy room with cards showing a clean room.

Doghouse

Materials: Doghouse and cards (pp. 123-125).

Preparation: Copy one doghouse (p.123) for every player, and cut apart the pieces for each doghouse; copy one set of cards and cut them apart (follow remaining preparation instructions on p.104).

Procedure: Each child chooses a card picturing a dog to use as a marker. Set the remaining dog cards aside. Mix doghouse cards and place facedown in a draw pile. Place the doghouse pieces faceup and spread out nearby. First player takes the top card from the draw pile and takes the corresponding piece from the doghouse pieces—a door, a wall, a roof or a triangle—and places it by his or her dog. Child places the doghouse card faceup to begin a discard pile. As play continues, children assemble doghouses. Play continues until each player has assembled a doghouse. (Note: Child takes a new doghouse piece only if he or she does not already have that piece on his or her doghouse.) When the draw pile is used up, the cards in the discard pile are mixed and then turned facedown and used as the draw pile.

For Younger Children: Each child chooses a card picturing a dog to use as a marker. Discard remaining cards. Copy an extra doghouse for every player (p. 123), which you leave whole as a doghouse pattern. Each player assembles a doghouse by laying the doghouse pieces on a doghouse pattern.

🌸 **Group Size:** One to four players

🌸 **Goal:** Collect pieces to build a doghouse.

Fly and Hop

Materials: Fly and Hop game cards (pp. 127-129).

Preparation: Make three copies of shape cards and one copy of action cards (prepare as instructed on p. 104). Clear an open playing area in the room.

Procedure: Show each action card and lead children in practicing the pictured motions. Place four different shape cards faceup on the floor, as far apart from each other as possible. Mix the other cards into two facedown piles—one of shape cards and one of action cards. Children stand near draw piles. First player takes a card from each of the draw piles and moves to that shape card using the designated action. Play continues until each child has had a turn or as time and interest allow.

For Younger Children: Do motions along with the children.

✿ **Group Size:** One to four players

✿ **Goal:** Identify shapes and move to them using fun actions.

Fruits and Vegetables

Materials: Fruits and Vegetables game boards (pp. 131-133).

Preparation: Make two copies of each game board, making each copy on a different color of card stock or copier paper; cut one copy of each game board into triangles as marked on game boards (follow remaining preparation instructions on p. 104).

Procedure: Mix triangles and place facedown as a draw pile. First player takes top card from pile and places it on a game board, covering the matching picture. Play continues until all triangles have been placed on the game boards.

For Older Children: Play without the game boards.

✿ **Group Size:** One to four players

✿ **Goal:** Match halves of fruits and vegetables.

I Spy

Materials: I Spy game boards 1 and 2 and cards (pp. 135-137).

Preparation: Make one copy of game boards and cards (prepare as instructed on p. 104). Keep game boards and cards in separate groups (see numbers on each game board and card).

Procedure: Arrange children in groups of up to four. Give each group an I Spy game board. Give each child in the group a card. Children look for objects on their game boards. When child sees the object, he or she calls out "I spy." When all objects have been found, collect game boards and cards. Groups trade game boards and cards. Play continues until each child has found each object or as time and interest allow.

Variation: Play a game like I Spy. Children form pairs or trios. First player calls out "I spy a (tree)." As each child sees the (tree) in the collage, child calls out "I spy."

✿ **Group Size:** One to eight players

✿ **Goal:** Find individual objects in a collage.

Picnic Race

Materials: Picnic Race game board and cards (pp. 139-141).

Preparation: Copy game board and cards (prepare as instructed on p. 104).

Procedure: Lay one example of each food game card faceup on a blank square on the game board. Mix the remaining cards and place them facedown near the game board as a draw pile. First player takes the top card. If it is an ant card, child places it on any of the food cards on the game board to show that the ants have "eaten" that food. If it is a food card not yet covered by an ant card, child takes the matching food card off the game board and keeps both cards. If it is a food card already covered by an ant, child places that food card faceup by the draw pile. Play continues until there is no food left to take off the picnic table.

For Younger Children: Play the game without the ant cards.

✿ **Group Size:** One to four players

✿ **Goal:** Help each other remove food items from the picnic table before the ants get the food.

Playground

Materials: Playground game board and cards (pp. 143-145), one game marker (button, toy animal or person, etc.) for each child.

Preparation: Make one copy of game board and two copies of cards (prepare as instructed on p. 104).

Procedure: Place action and number cards in two separate facedown piles. Each player places a game marker near the "1" on the game board. First player takes a card from the action pile (help with reading as necessary). Child completes the action and then takes a card from the other pile to move game marker the appropriate number of spaces. Play continues until all players reach the "6" on the game board or until time is called. (Note: If a player reaches "6" before the other players, he or she continues to take action cards but does not move game marker.)

 Group Size: One to four players

 Goal: Finish game board course by doing physical actions listed on cards.

Pyramid

Materials: Pyramid game board and building pieces (p. 147) and cards (p. 149).

Preparation: Make two copies of game board and building pieces, making each copy on a different color of card stock or copier paper; copy one set of cards (follow remaining preparation instructions on p. 104). Keep the game board from one color and the building pieces from the other color. Discard remaining pieces and game board.

Procedure: Place the game board faceup with the triangle at the top. Place the game cards facedown as a draw pile. Lay the building pieces faceup so that each one is visible. First player takes the top card from the draw pile, finds a matching building piece and places building piece onto the corresponding shape on the game board. Then child places the game card at the bottom of the draw pile. Play continues until each shape on the pyramid has been covered with a building piece or as time and interest allow.

For Older Children: A child adds a building piece to the game board only if the building piece fits on the bottom row or touches the top of another building piece.

 Group Size: One to four players

 Goal: Help each other build a pyramid by stacking diamonds, triangles and trapezoids.

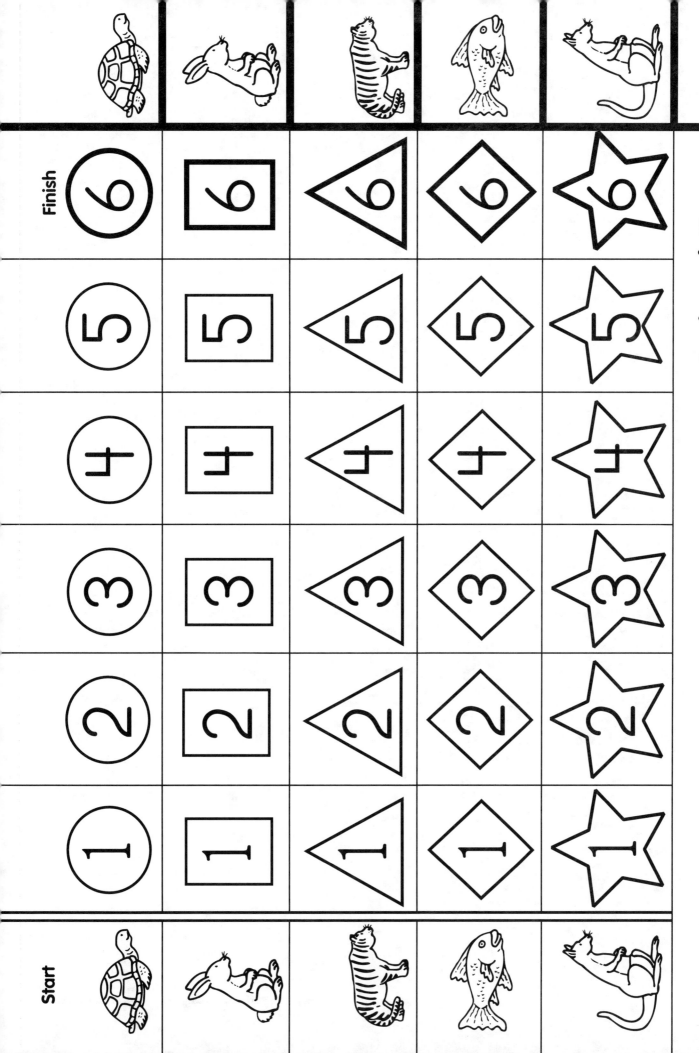

Animal Race

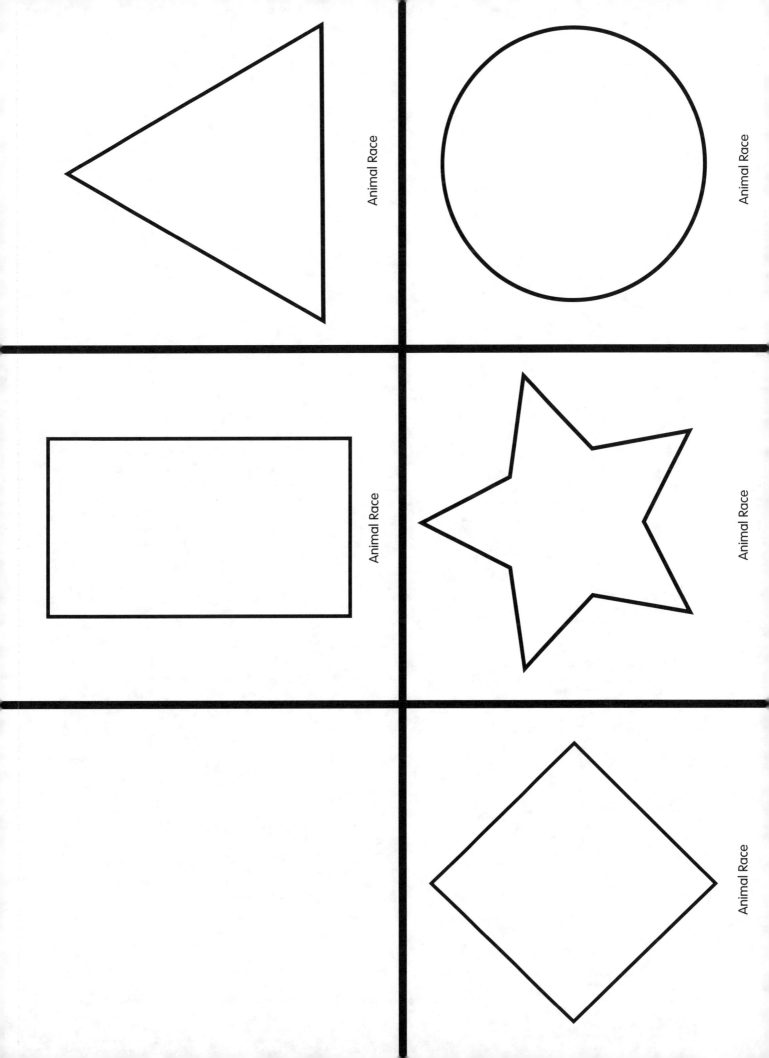

Animal Race

Animal Race

Animal Race

Animal Race

Animal Race

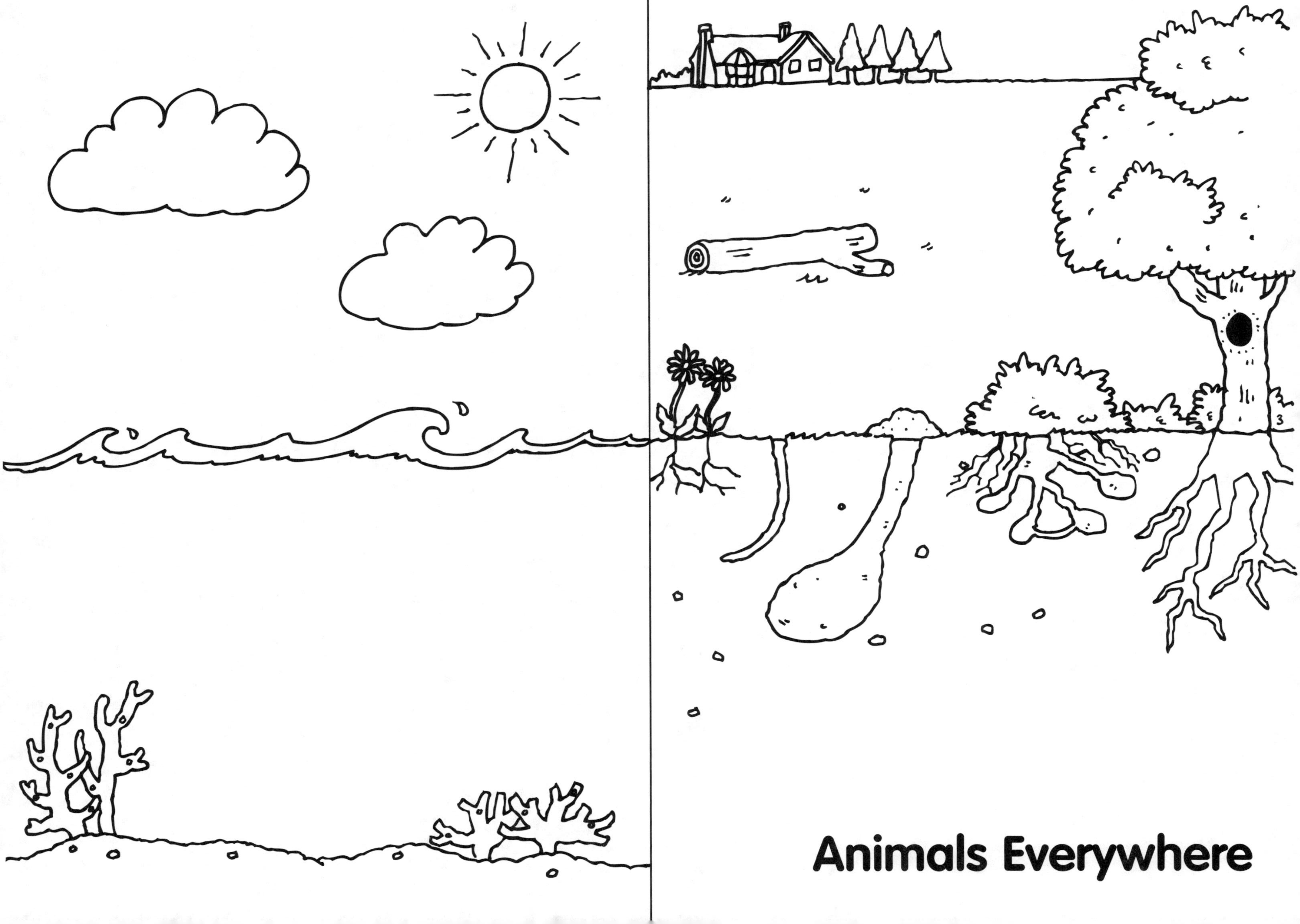

Animals Everywhere

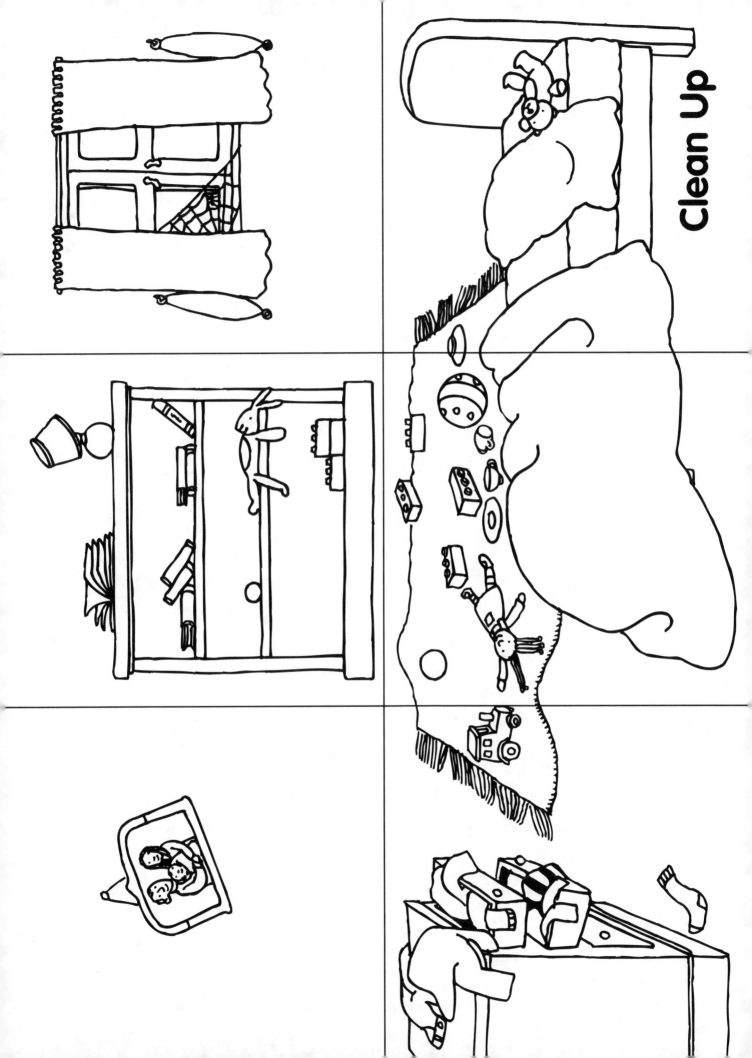

Clean Up

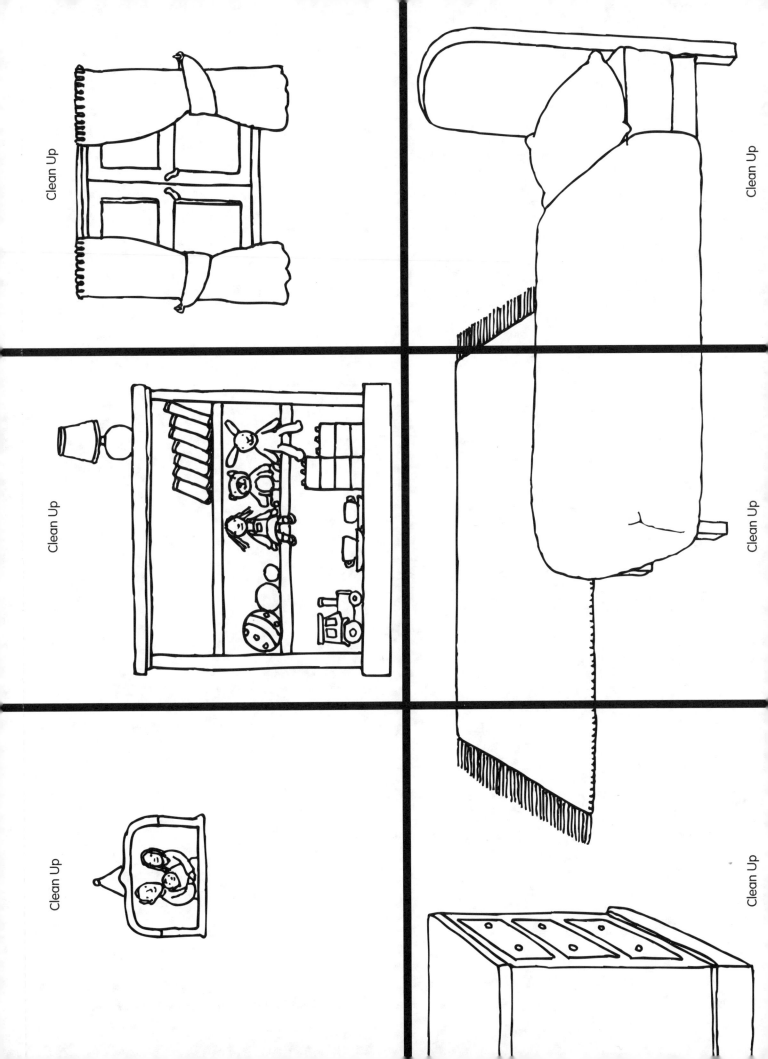

Clean Up

Clean Up

Clean Up

Clean Up

Clean Up

Clean Up

Doghouse

Doghouse

Doghouse

Doghouse

Doghouse

Doghouse

Doghouse

Doghouse

Doghouse

Doghouse

Doghouse

Doghouse

Doghouse

Doghouse

Doghouse

Doghouse

Fly and Hop

Fly and Hop

Fly and Hop

Fly and Hop

Big Steps
Fly and Hop

Crawl
Fly and Hop

Tiptoe
Fly and Hop

Ski (Slide Feet)
Fly and Hop

Hop
Fly and Hop

Walk Backwards
Fly and Hop

Fly
Fly and Hop

Swim
Fly and Hop

Fruits and Vegetables

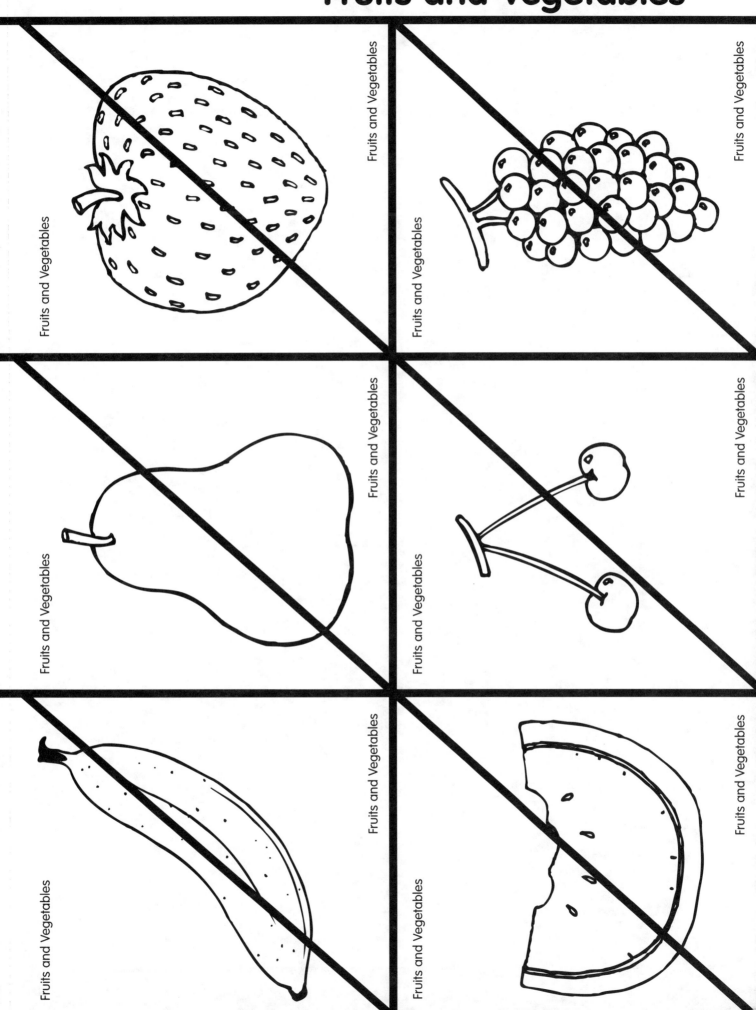

Fruits and Vegetables

Fruits and Vegetables

Fruits and Vegetables

Fruits and Vegetables

Fruits and Vegetables

Fruits and Vegetables

Fruits and Vegetables

Fruits and Vegetables

Fruits and Vegetables

Fruits and Vegetables

Fruits and Vegetables

Fruits and Vegetables

Fruits and Vegetables

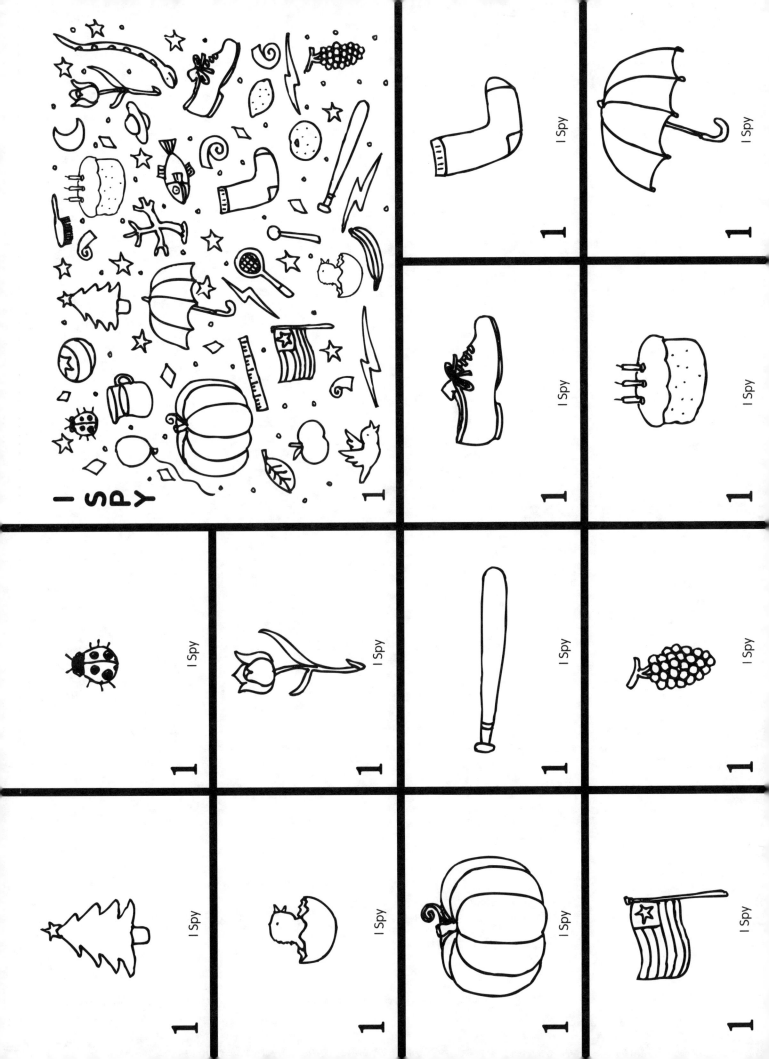

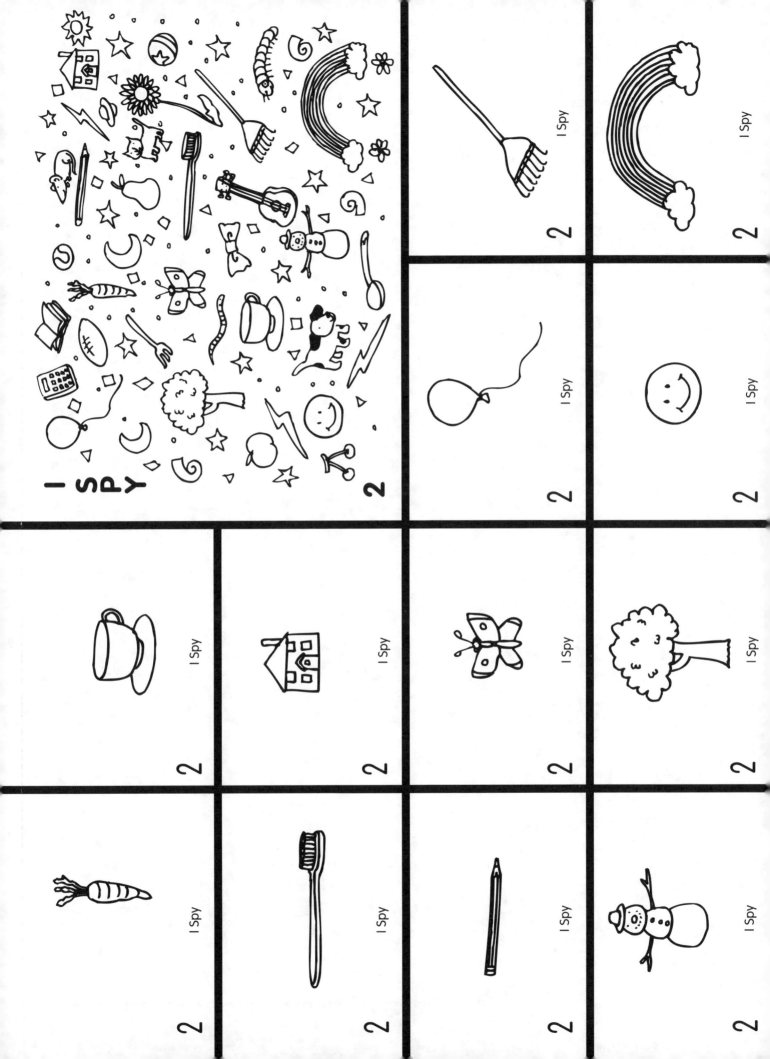

I SPY

2

I Spy 2

I Spy 2

I Spy 2

I Spy 2

I Spy 2

I Spy 2

I Spy 2

I Spy 2

I Spy 2

I Spy 2

I Spy 2

Picnic Race

Picnic Race

Picnic Race

Picnic Race

Picnic Race

Picnic Race

Picnic Race

Picnic Race

Picnic Race

Picnic Race

Picnic Race

Picnic Race

Picnic Race

Picnic Race

Picnic Race

Picnic Race

Picnic Race

Picnic Race

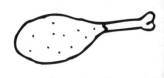

Picnic Race

Picnic Race

Picnic Race

Playground

Turn around 3 times. Playground

Touch toes. Playground

Clap 2 times. Playground

Blink. Playground

Hop on 1 foot. Playground

1 Playground · 1 Playground · 1 Playground · 1 Playground · 1 Playground

2 Playground · 2 Playground · 1 Playground · 1 Playground · 1 Playground

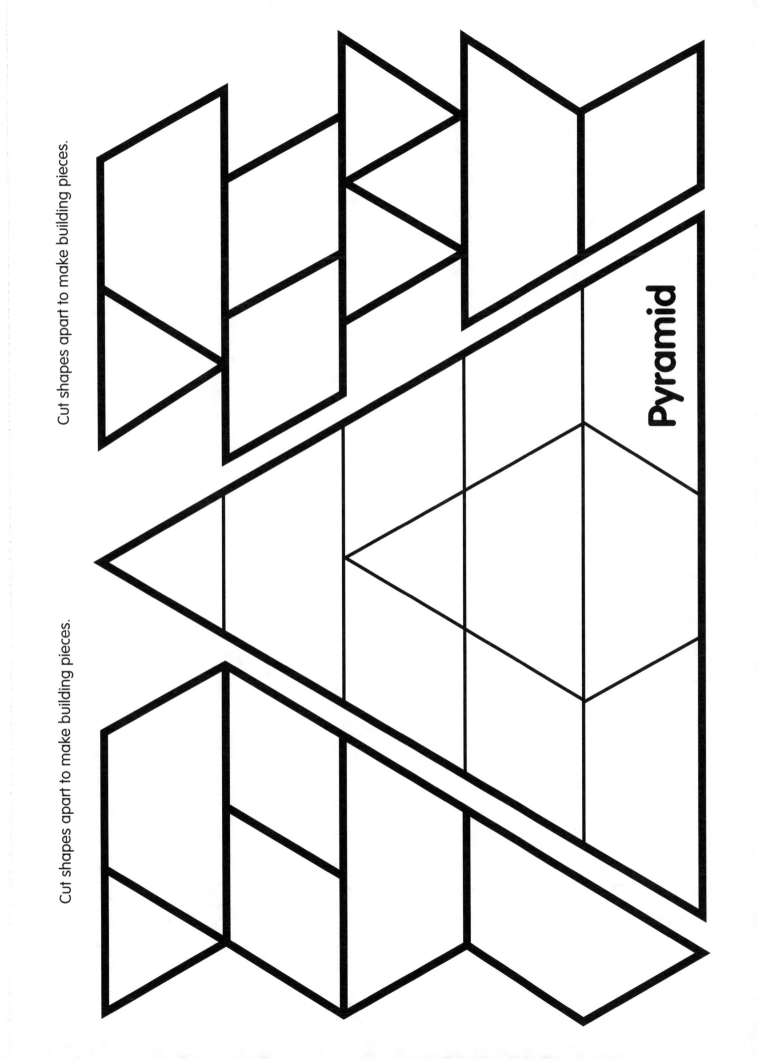

Cut shapes apart to make building pieces.

Cut shapes apart to make building pieces.

Pyramid

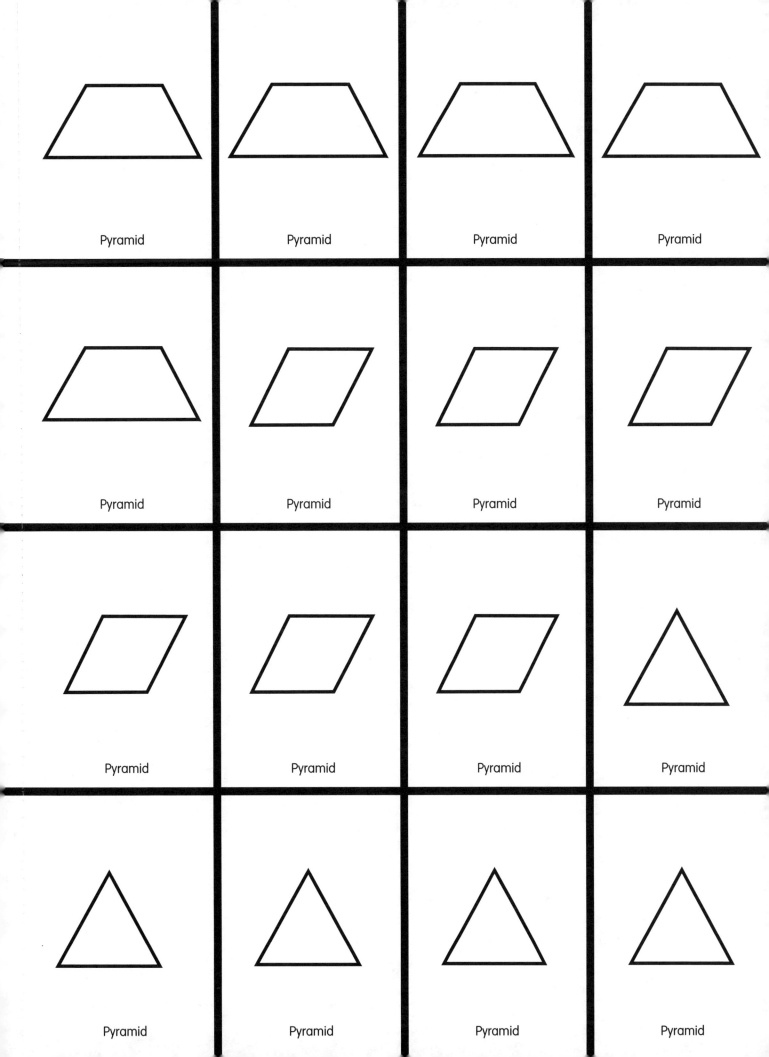

Pyramid

Pyramid

Pyramid

Pyramid

Pyramid

Pyramid

Pyramid

Pyramid

Pyramid

Pyramid

Pyramid

Pyramid

Pyramid

Pyramid

Pyramid

Pyramid

Puppet Activities

Children will love playing—and learning—with these puppets. The versatile and easy-to-use puppets include people, animals and even child and adult vehicles. The suggested activities will allow you to effectively use puppets in any lesson or as free play. (To use backdrops with puppets, see Puppet Play on p. 202.)

HOW to Prepare the Puppets

☺ Photocopy the puppets (pp. 157-197).

☺ Cut pages apart along the heavy lines using a paper cutter or scissors.

☺ Prefold puppets.

☺ For a handy collection of puppets, save puppets and a copy of the activity directions in an envelope, folder or resealable plastic bag.

Animals at Play

Materials: Animals puppets (pp. 157-175), markers or crayons, transparent tape; optional—if children will be making stick puppets, provide a craft stick or ruler or straw for each puppet.

Preparation: Choose two to four puppets appropriate for your play. Copy the puppet pages, making enough copies so that each child will have one or two puppets (prepare as instructed on p. 152).

Procedure: Children color puppets. Children fold puppets. Help children tape the front and back sides of puppets together. (Optional: If using Stick Puppets, children help tape puppets to craft sticks, rulers or straws.)

Children use their puppets to act like animals playing outdoors. Ask questions such as:

- **How would a bear and a squirrel play Follow the Leader?**

- **What would animals do if they were playing Hide and Seek?**

- **What would your animals do at the beach?**

- **What would it sound like if animals tried to sing together?**

Variation: Use a Play Scene such as Beach, (pp. 203-205) Forest, (pp. 219-221) Garden, (pp. 223-225) Mountain Meadow, (pp. 227-229) or Sea (pp. 231-233) as a backdrop.

Bible Story Review

Materials: People puppets (pp. 185-191), markers or crayons, transparent tape; optional—if children will be making stick puppets, provide a craft stick or ruler or straw for each puppet.

Preparation: Choose two to four puppets appropriate for a Bible story with which children are familiar, making enough copies so that each child will have one or two puppets (prepare as instructed on p.152).

Procedure: Children color puppets. Children fold puppets. Help children tape the front and back sides of puppets together. (Optional: If using Stick Puppets, children help tape puppets to craft sticks, rulers or straws.)

Children use the puppets to act out the Bible story. To help children recall Bible story action, ask questions such as:

- **Who was in the Bible story?**

- **Where were they?**

- **What did they do?**

- **What did they say?**

- **What happened first?**

- **What happened next?**

- **How did the story end?**

To begin, you may need to say the story dialogue. As children practice acting out the story, however, they will enjoy providing the dialogue.

Let's Go on a Trip

Materials: People and Vehicle puppets (pp. 185-197), markers or crayons, transparent tape; optional—if children will be making stick puppets, provide a craft stick or ruler or straw for each puppet.

Preparation: Choose two to four puppets appropriate for your play. Copy the puppet pages, making enough copies so that each child will have one or two puppets (prepare as instructed on p. 152).

Procedure: Children color puppets. Children fold puppets. Help children tape the front and back sides of puppets together. (Optional: If using Stick Puppets, children help tape puppets to craft sticks, rulers or straws.)

Children use puppets to act out preparing for a trip and then some things they will do on their trip. Ask questions such as:

- **Where is some place you like to go in a car?**

- **Have you ever gone on a plane? Where did you go?**

- **If you visit your grandparents, what things do you take with you?**

- **What will you do on your trip? What will you see?**

Life Application Play

Materials: Puppets (pp. 157-197), markers or crayons, transparent tape; optional—if children will be making stick puppets, provide a craft stick or ruler or straw for each puppet.

Preparation: Choose two to four puppets appropriate for showing ways to obey a Bible verse. Copy the puppet pages, making enough copies so that each child will have one or two puppets (prepare as instructed on p. 152).

Procedure: Children color puppets. Children fold puppets. Help children tape the front and back sides of puppets together. (Optional: If using Stick Puppets, children help tape puppets to craft sticks, rulers or straws.)

Read a Bible verse aloud to children. Help children use puppets to act out ways of obeying the verse. Introduce activity with comments such as:

- **Today we are talking about ways to (obey God).**

- **One way to (obey God) is to (take turns).**

- **What could your puppets do to (take turns)?**

- **One way to (obey God) is to (help someone who is hurt).**

- **What could your puppets do to (help someone)?**

Choose from These Verses:
"Do what is right and good." Deuteronomy 6:18
"Obey the Lord." Deuteronomy 27:10
"God, we give you thanks." 1 Chronicles 29:13
"A friend loves at all times." Proverbs 17:17
"Love one another." John 13:34
"Share with God's people who are in need." Romans 12:13
"Always try to be kind to each other." 1 Thessalonians 5:15

Singing Puppets

Materials: Faces and People puppets (pp. 177-191), markers or crayons, transparent tape, children's music cassette/CD and player; optional—if children will be making stick puppets, provide a craft stick or ruler or straw for each puppet.

Preparation: Choose two to four puppets appropriate for your play. Copy the puppet pages, making enough copies so that each child will have one or two puppets (prepare as instructed on p. 152).

Procedure: Children color puppets. Children fold puppets. Help children tape the front and back sides of puppets together. (Optional: If using Stick Puppets, children help tape puppets to craft sticks, rulers or straws.)

Play song from children's music cassette/CD. Children move puppets to pretend they are singing. As children become familiar with the song, they may sing along.

Variation: Children suggest a favorite song to sing.

What Do You Like to Do?

Materials: Puppets (pp. 157-197), markers or crayons, transparent tape; optional—if children will be making stick puppets, provide a craft stick or ruler or straw for each puppet.

Preparation: Choose two to four puppets appropriate for your play. Copy the puppet pages, making enough copies so that each child will have one or two puppets (prepare as instructed on p. 152).

Procedure: Children color puppets. Children fold puppets. Help children tape the front and back sides of puppets together. (Optional: If using Stick Puppets, children help tape puppets to craft sticks, rulers or straws.)

Children use their puppets to act out things they like to do. Ask questions such as:

• **What do you like to do at the park?**

• **What's your favorite game to play?**

• **What do you like to do outside?**

• **What do you like to do with your friends?**

• **What's a fun place you like to go with your dad or mom?**

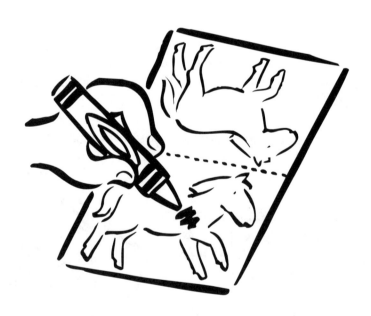

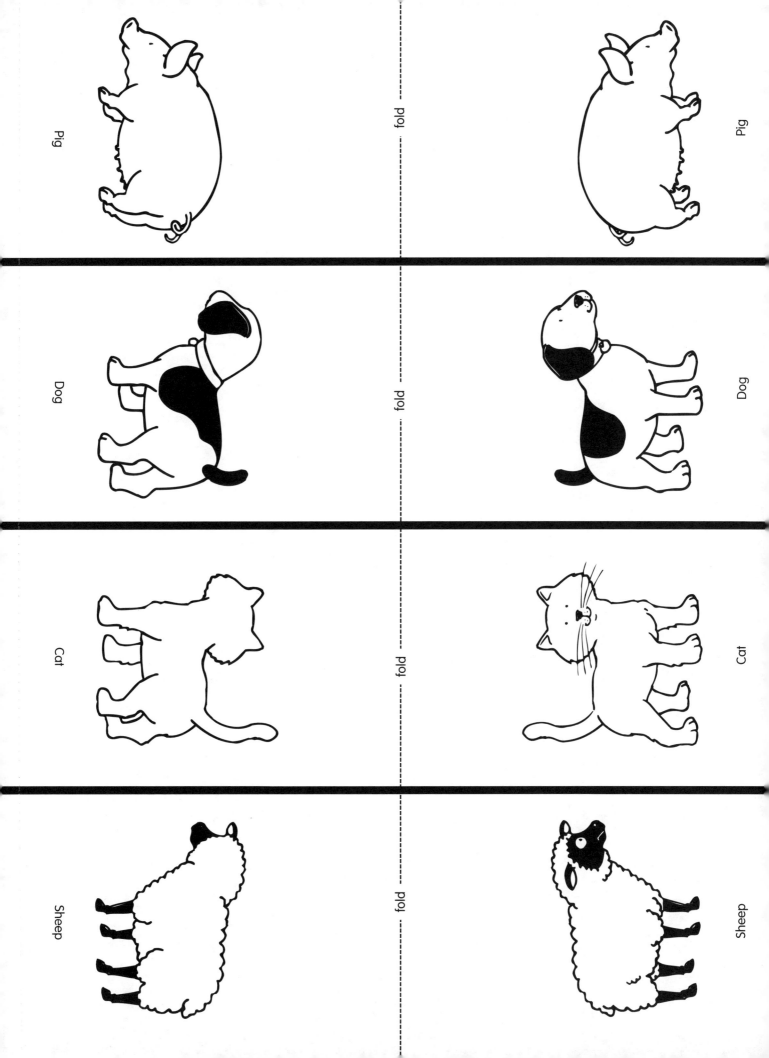

Pig

Pig

fold

Dog

Dog

fold

Cat

Cat

fold

Sheep

Sheep

fold

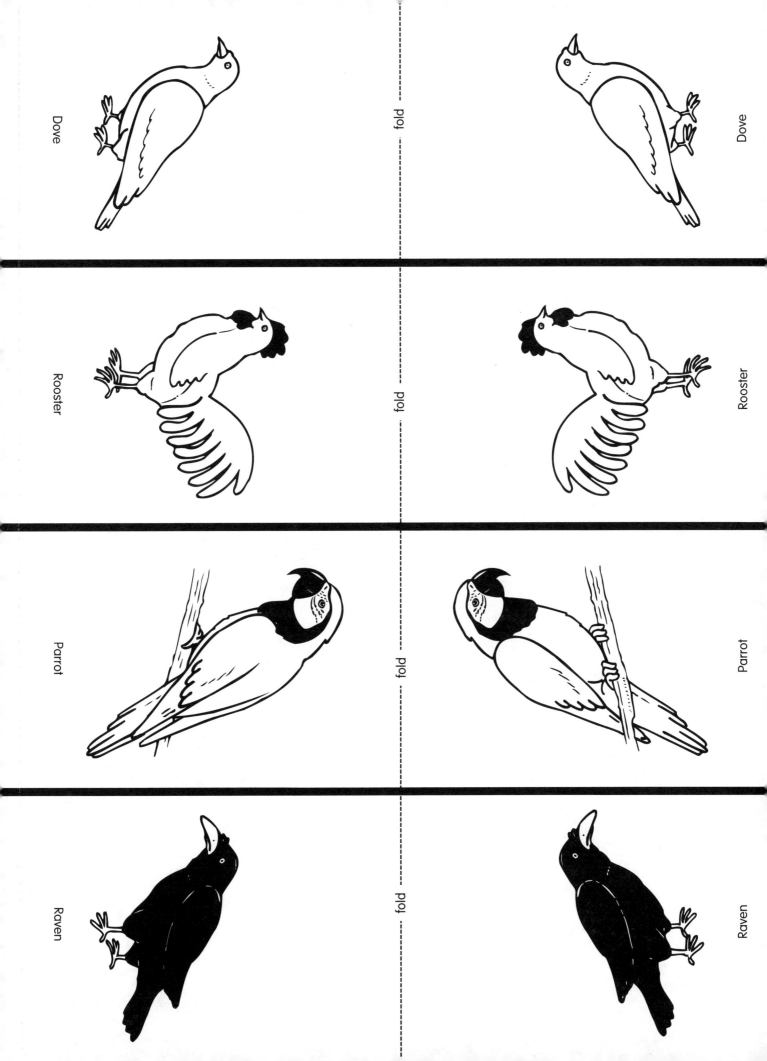

Dove

Dove

fold

Rooster

Rooster

fold

Parrot

Parrot

fold

Raven

Raven

fold

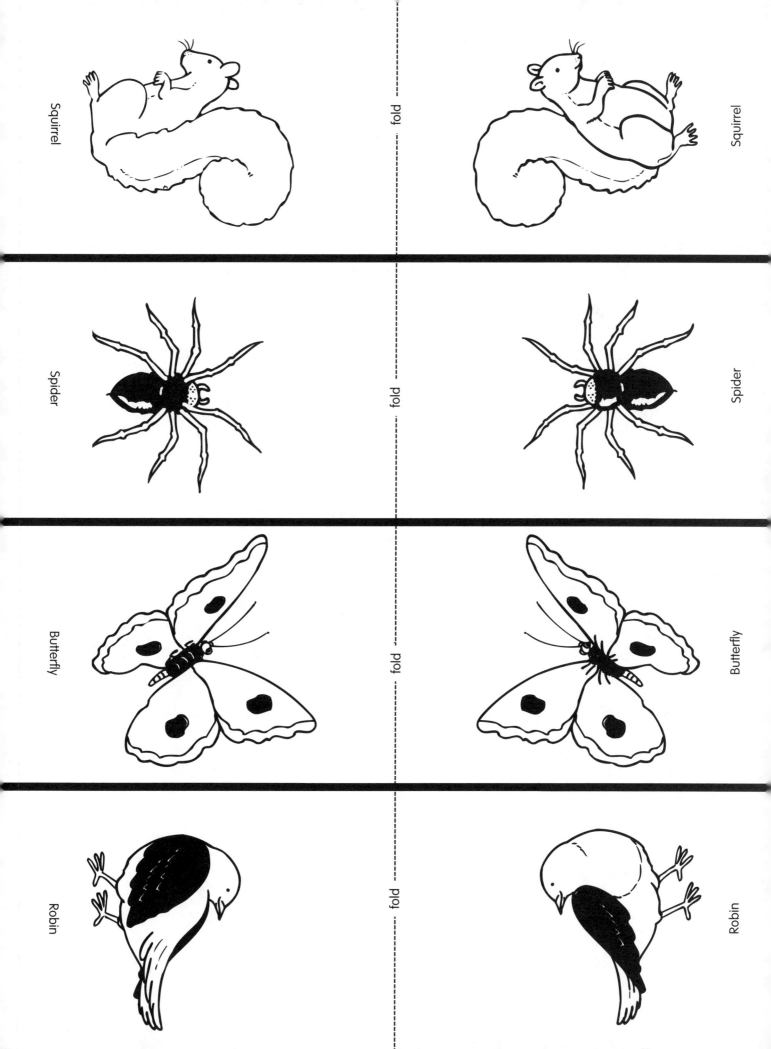

Squirrel

fold

Squirrel

Spider

fold

Spider

Butterfly

fold

Butterfly

Robin

fold

Robin

Penguin

Penguin

fold

Frog

Frog

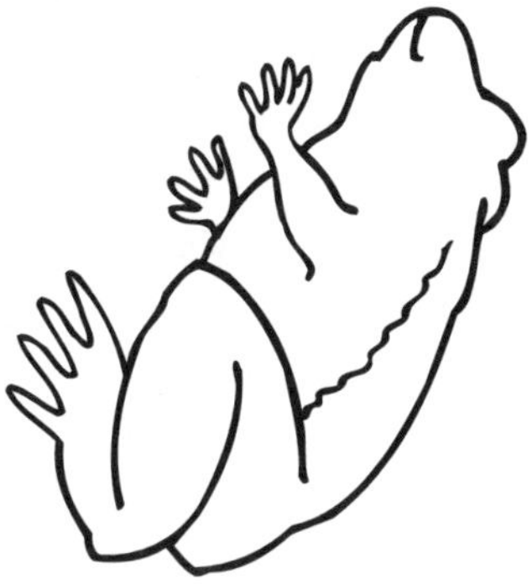

fold

Trout

Trout

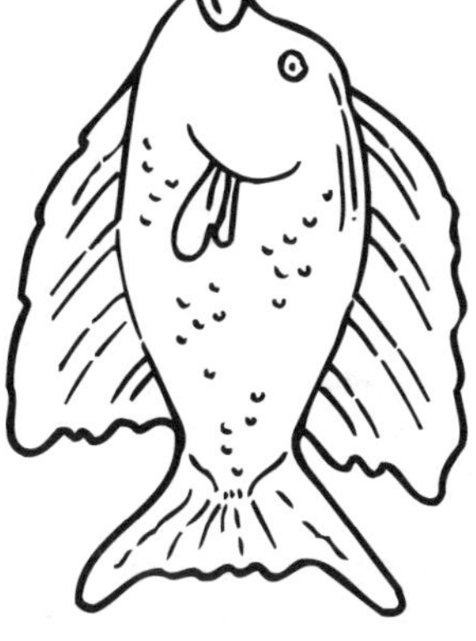

fold

Angelfish

Angelfish

fold

Horse

Horse

Horse

fold

Cow

Cow

fold

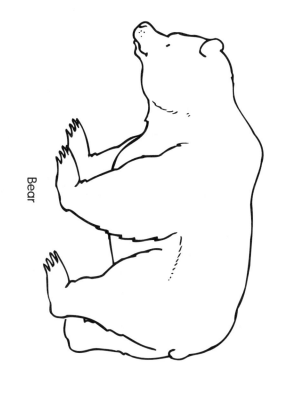

Bear

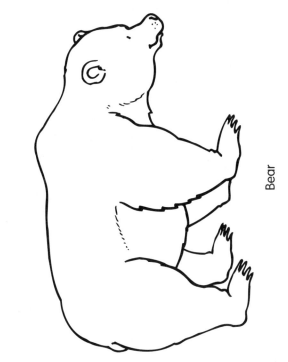

Bear

fold

Kangaroo

Kangaroo

fold

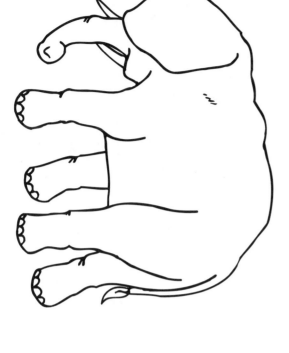

Elephant

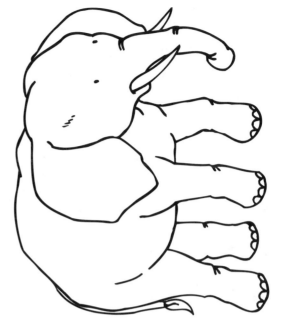

Elephant

fold

Zebra

Zebra

fold

Lion

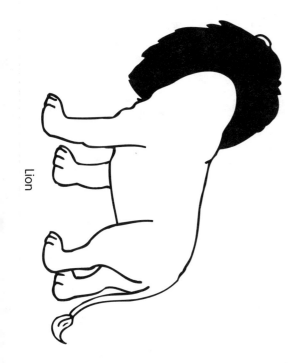

Lion

fold

Tiger

Tiger

fold

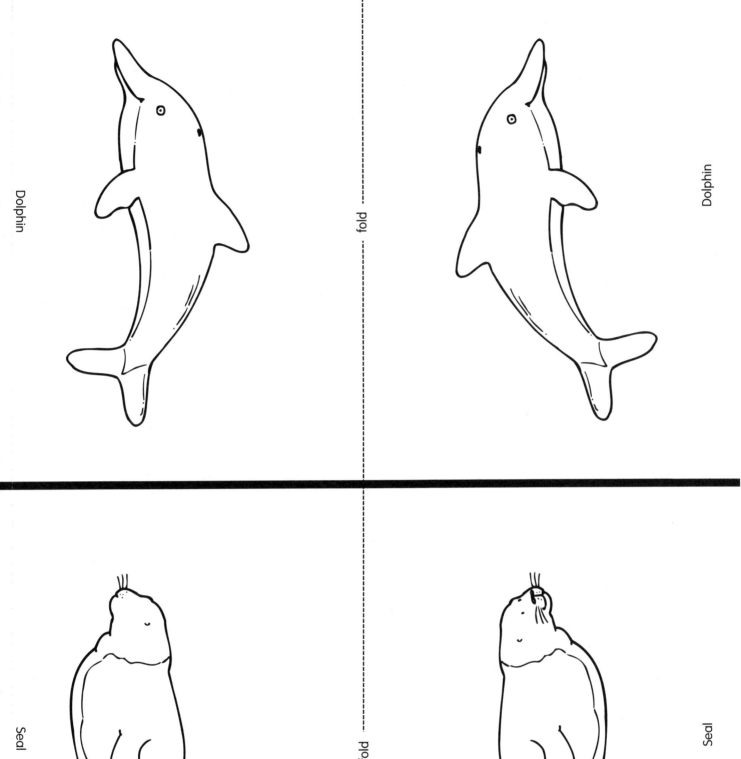

Dolphin

Dolphin

fold

Seal

fold

Seal

Whale

fold

Whale

Shark

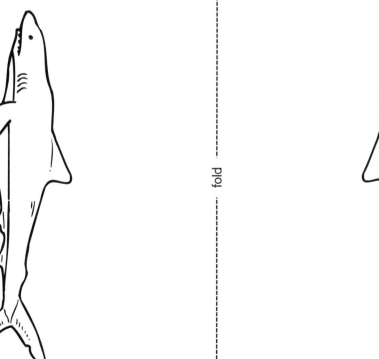

fold

Shark

Toddler

Jesus

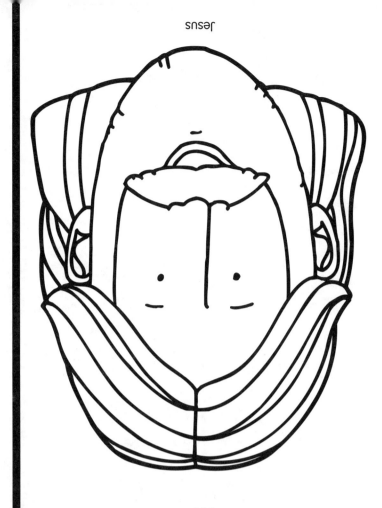

------------------------------ fold ------------------------------ fold ------------------------------

Toddler

Jesus

Boy

Girl

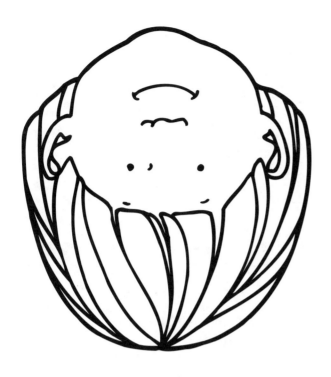

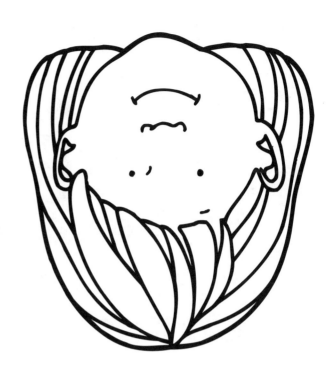

------- fold ------- ------- fold -------

Boy

Girl

Boy

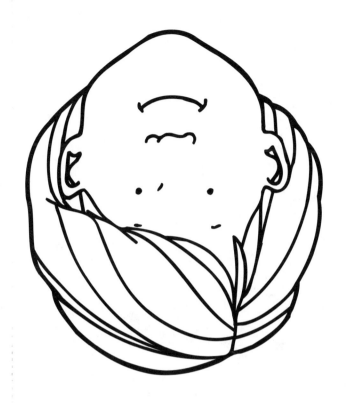

Girl

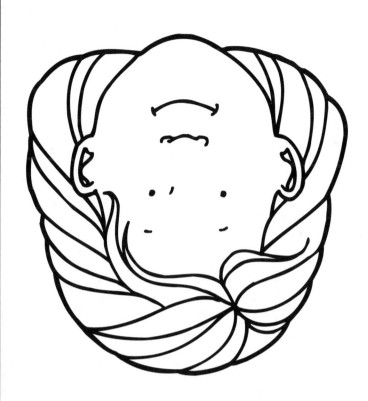

------------------------------ fold ----------------------------------- fold ------------------------------

Boy

Girl

Man

Woman

fold

fold

Man

Woman

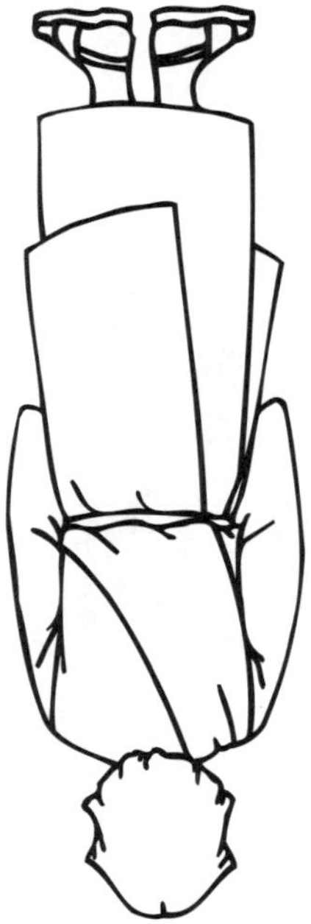

Bible-Times Boy

Bible-Times Boy

Bible-Times Girl

Bible-Times Girl

Bible-Times Toddler

Bible-Times Toddler

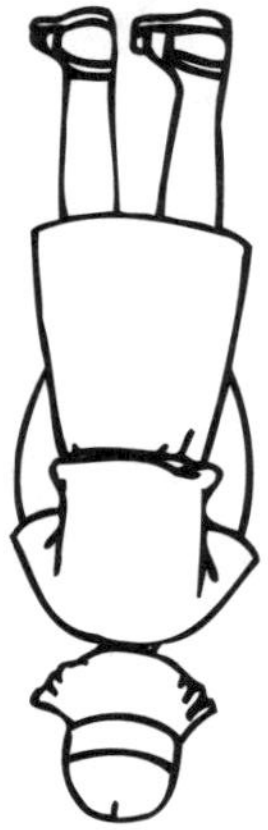

Jesus

Jesus

fold

fold

fold

fold

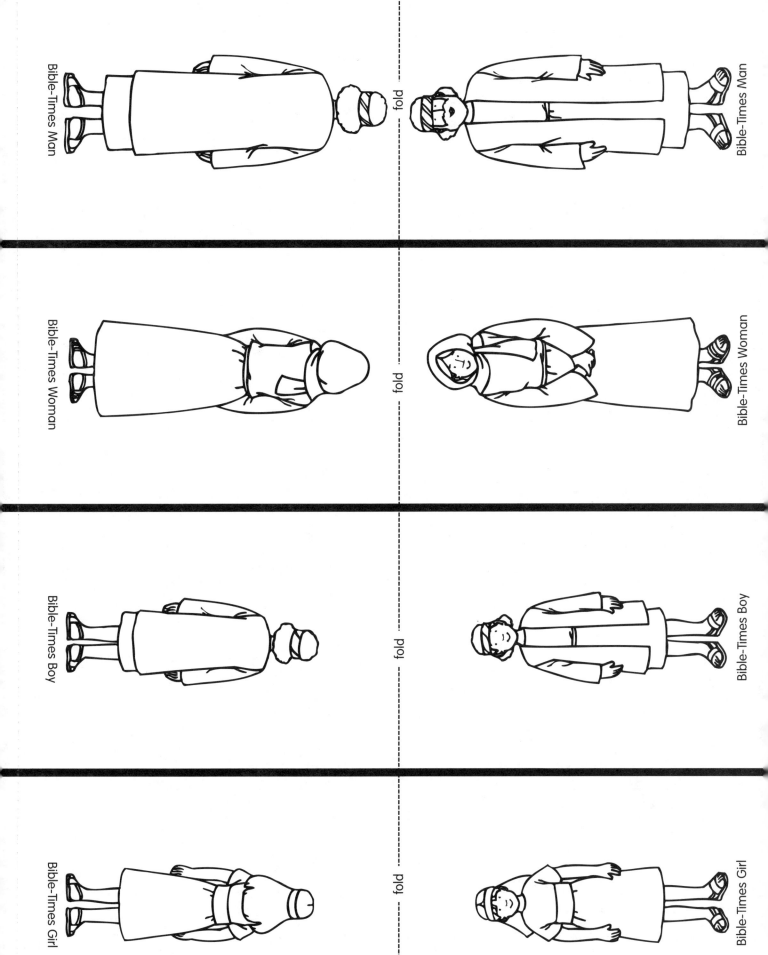

Bible-Times Man

Bible-Times Man

Bible-Times Woman

Bible-Times Woman

Bible-Times Boy

Bible-Times Boy

Bible-Times Girl

Bible-Times Girl

fold

fold

fold

fold

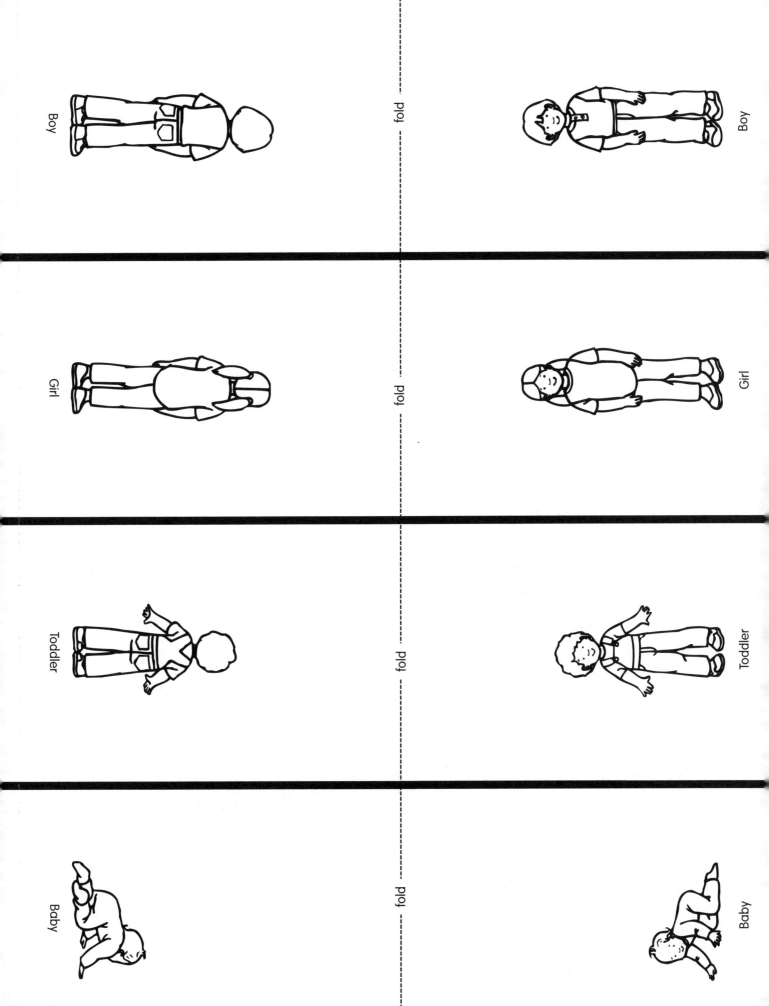

Boy

Boy

fold

Girl

Girl

fold

Toddler

Toddler

fold

Baby

Baby

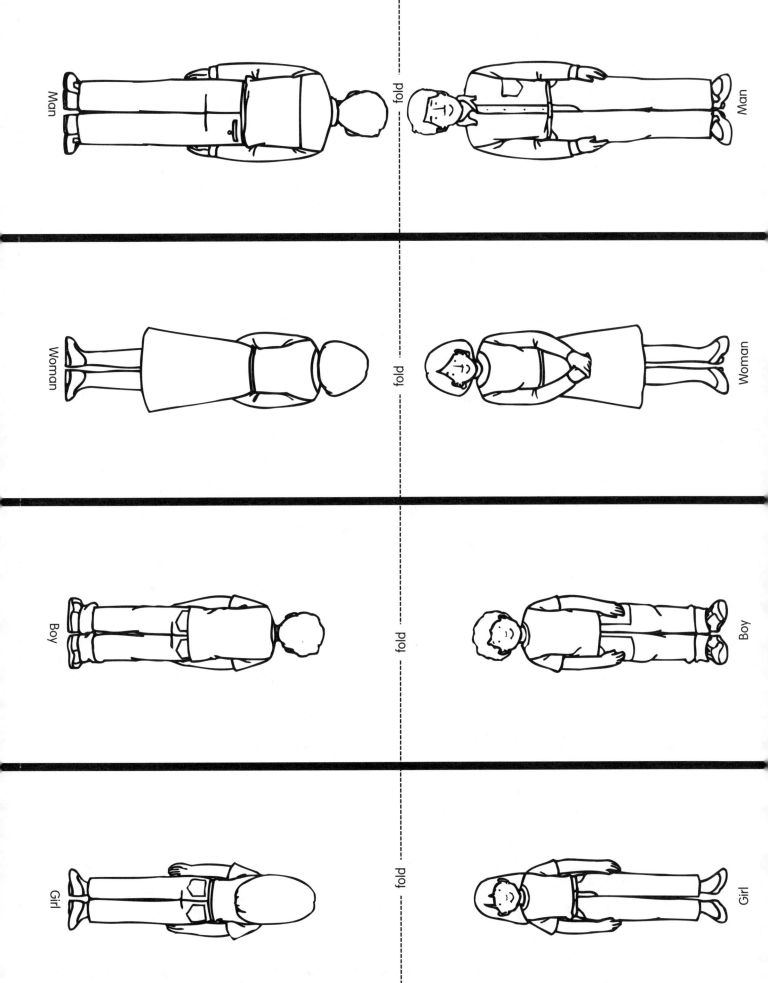

Man

Man

fold

Woman

Woman

fold

Boy

Boy

fold

Girl

Girl

fold

Bible-Times Boat

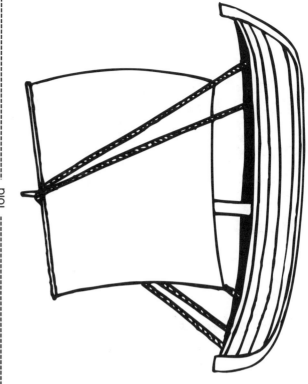

Bible-Times Boat

fold

fold

Noah's Ark

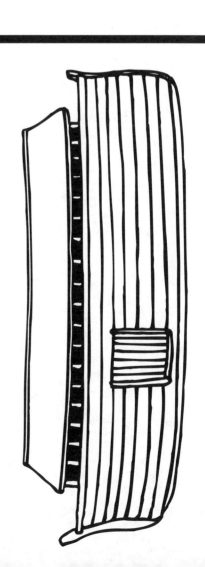

Noah's Ark

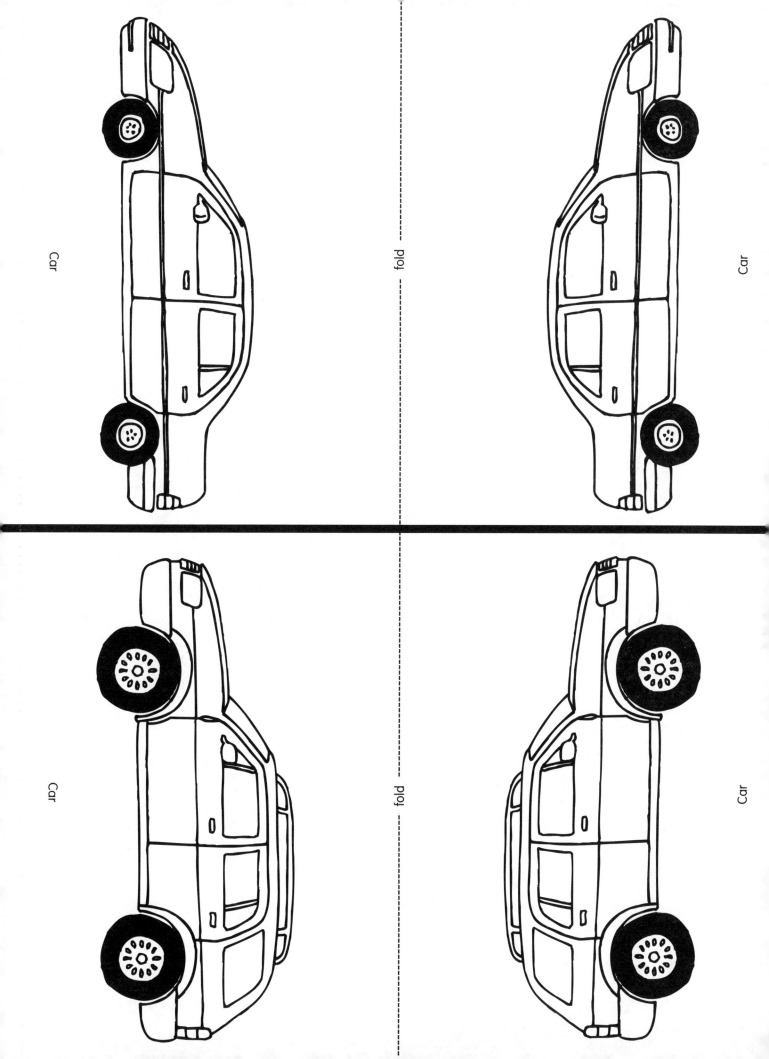

Car

Car

fold

fold

Car

Car

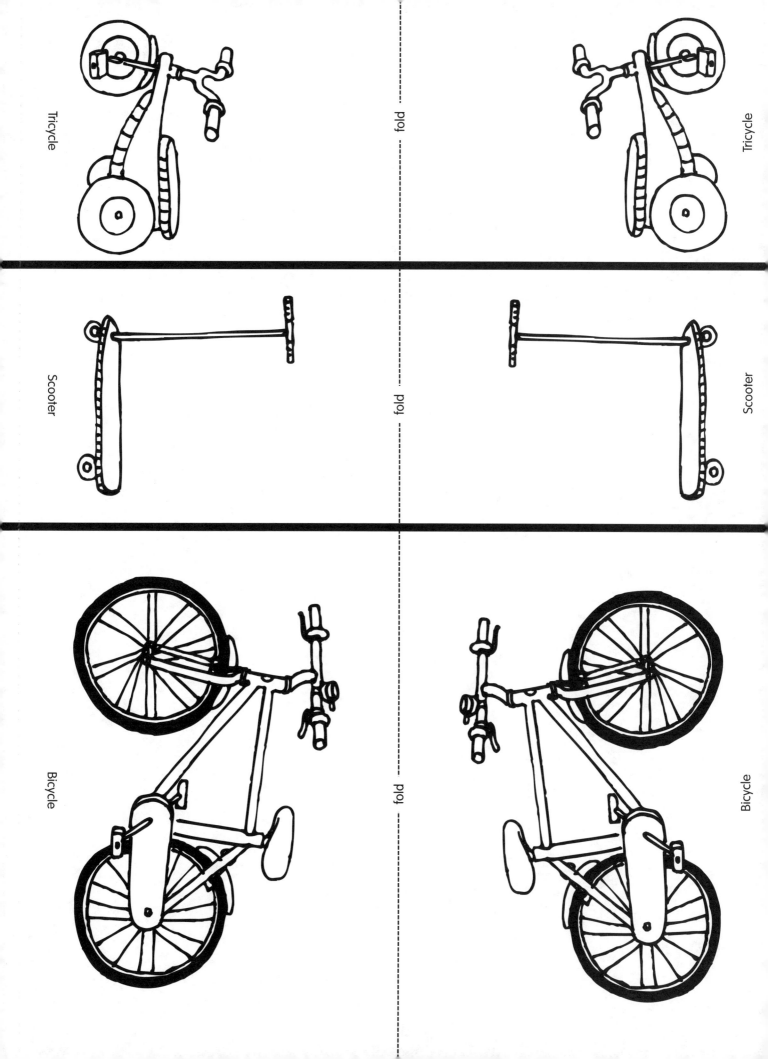

Tricycle

Tricycle

fold

Scooter

Scooter

fold

Bicycle

Bicycle

fold

Play Scenes

Children can use these scenes to act out favorite Bible stories or contemporary situations. This can be done either with the puppets from the preceding section or with toys. These scenes are also ready to use for creative art and nature activities. The scenes can even be enlarged so that children can create hands-on wall murals.

HOW to Prepare Play Scenes

☼ Photocopy pages (pp. 203-233) onto white copier paper or card stock.

☼ Each page goes with another page to form a two-page scene. The first page of each of these pairs is marked as the "Left page" and the second as the "Right page." First allow the children to color the pages. Then tape pages together.

☺ For a handy collection of scenes, save each page with a copy of the activity directions in an envelope, folder or resealable plastic bag.

Art Play

Materials: One pair of play scene pages for each child or for every two children (prepare as instructed on p. 200), collage items (chenille wire, raffia, buttons, fabric, tissue paper, etc.), glue, tape.

Procedure: Children decorate pages by gluing art materials onto them. Tape pages together.

Variation: Enlarge scene onto butcher paper with an overhead projector to create a mural. Children decorate mural.

Block Play

Materials: One pair of play scene pages for every two children (prepare as instructed on p. 200); crayons, colored markers or colored pencils; tape; toys that correlate with scene; blocks.

Procedure: Children color pages. Tape pages together and place on table or floor. Children play with toys and blocks on play mat.

Variation: Provide puppets (pp. 157-197) as stand-up toys, without taping sides together.

Coloring Play

Materials: One or two pages of a scene for each child (prepare as instructed on p. 200); crayons, colored markers or colored pencils; tape.

Procedure: Children color pages.

Variation: Children draw additional items on coloring pages before coloring them.

Nature Play

Materials: One pair of play scene pages for each child or for every two children (prepare as instructed on p. 200), nature items (dry beans, popcorn, sunflower seeds, leaves, sticks, moss, berries, seeds, bark, feathers, orange rind, etc.), glue, tape.

Procedure: Children decorate pages by gluing nature materials onto them. Tape pages together.

Variation: Enlarge scene onto butcher paper with an overhead projector to create a mural. Children decorate mural.

Puppet Play

Materials: One pair of play scene pages for every two children (prepare as instructed on p. 200); crayons, colored markers or colored pencils; tape; cardboard boxes.

Procedure: Children color play scenes. Tape pages together. Lay scene on a flat surface or affix scene to the side of a cardboard box, to a bulletin board or to a wall. Lead children in one of the activities listed under Puppets (choose from pp. 153-156).

Choose from These Play Scenes: Sea (pp. 231-233) for "Jesus Stops the Storm," Bible-Times Land (pp. 207-209) for "The Good Samaritan," Garden (pp. 223-225) for "God Made Animals," Forest (pp. 219-221) or Mountain Meadow (pp. 227-229) for "Loading the Big Boat," Beach (pp. 203-205) or Sea (pp. 231-233) for "Jonah and the Big Fish," etc.

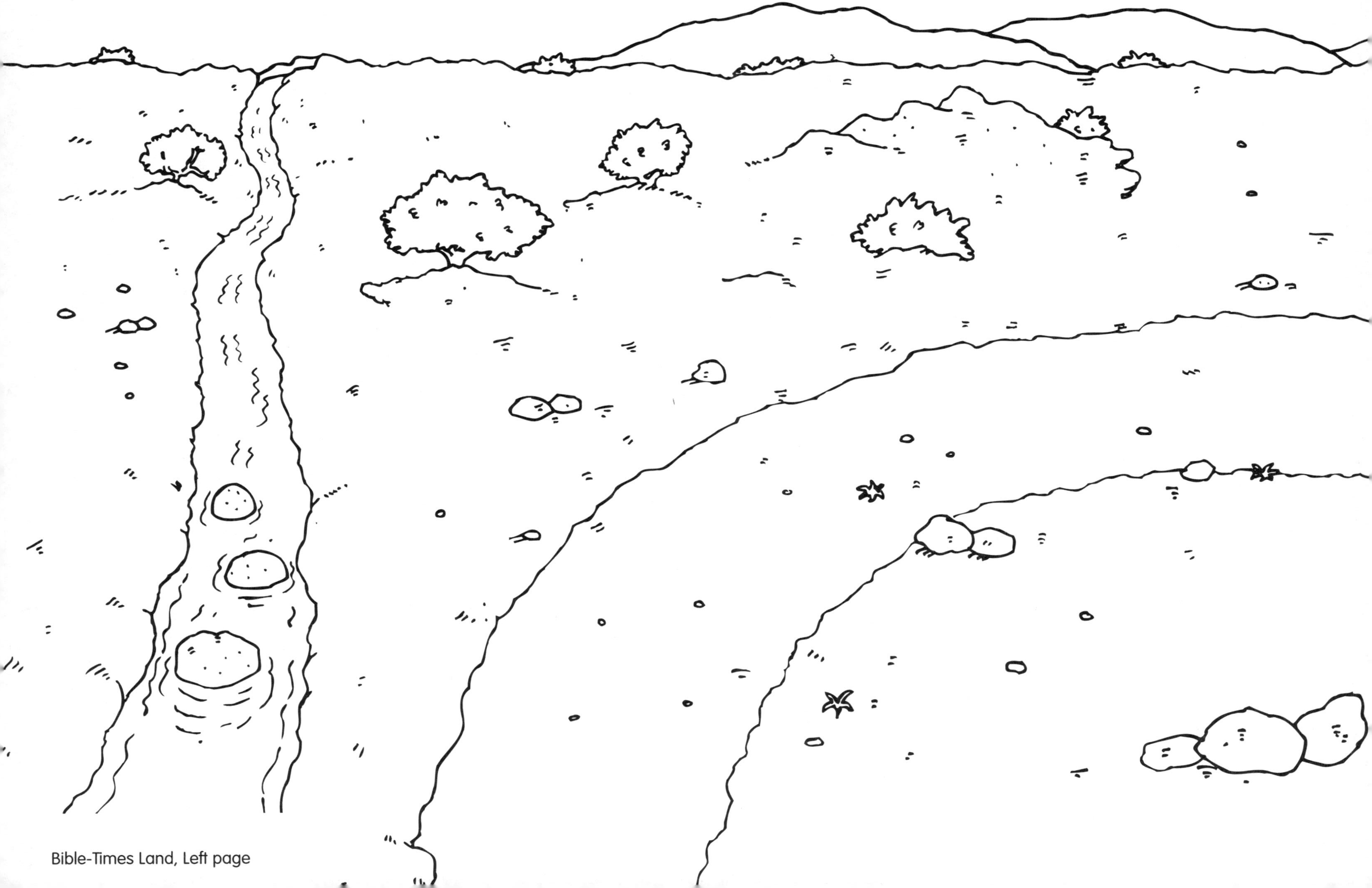

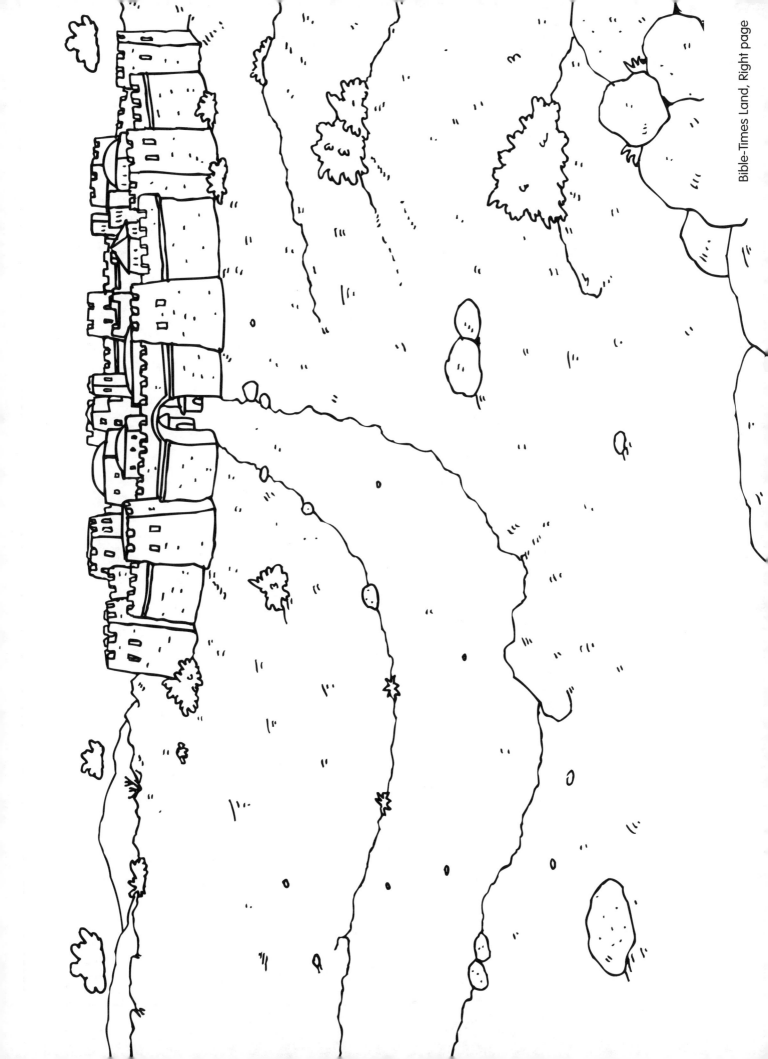

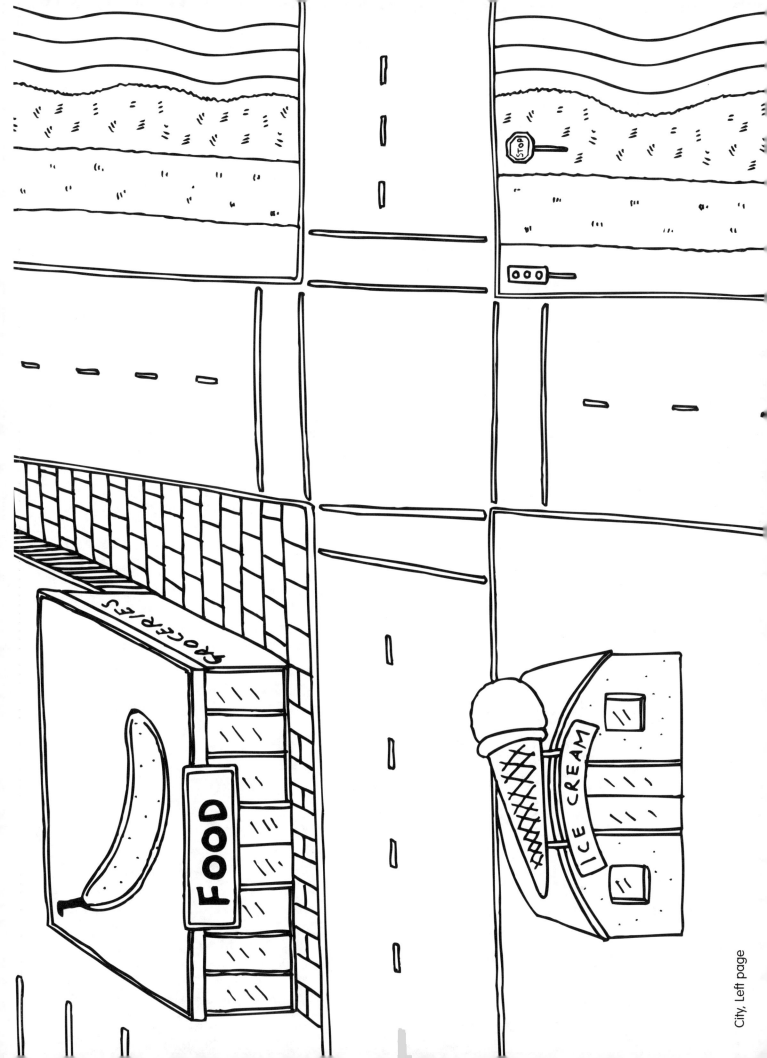

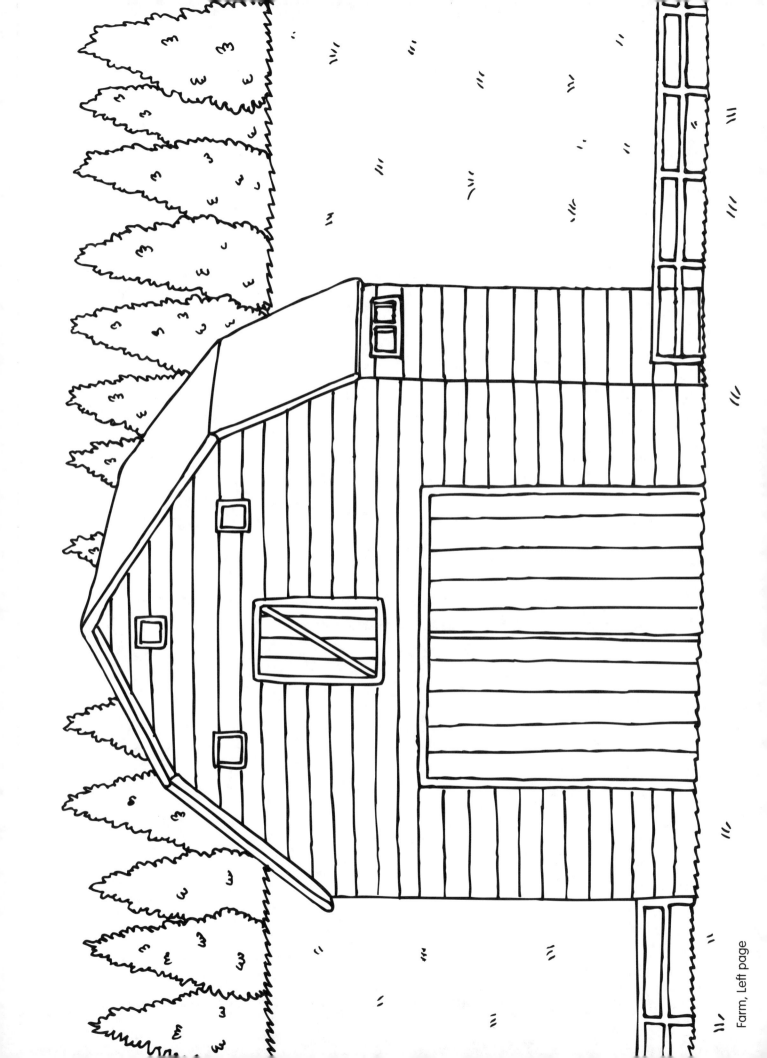

Farm, Left page

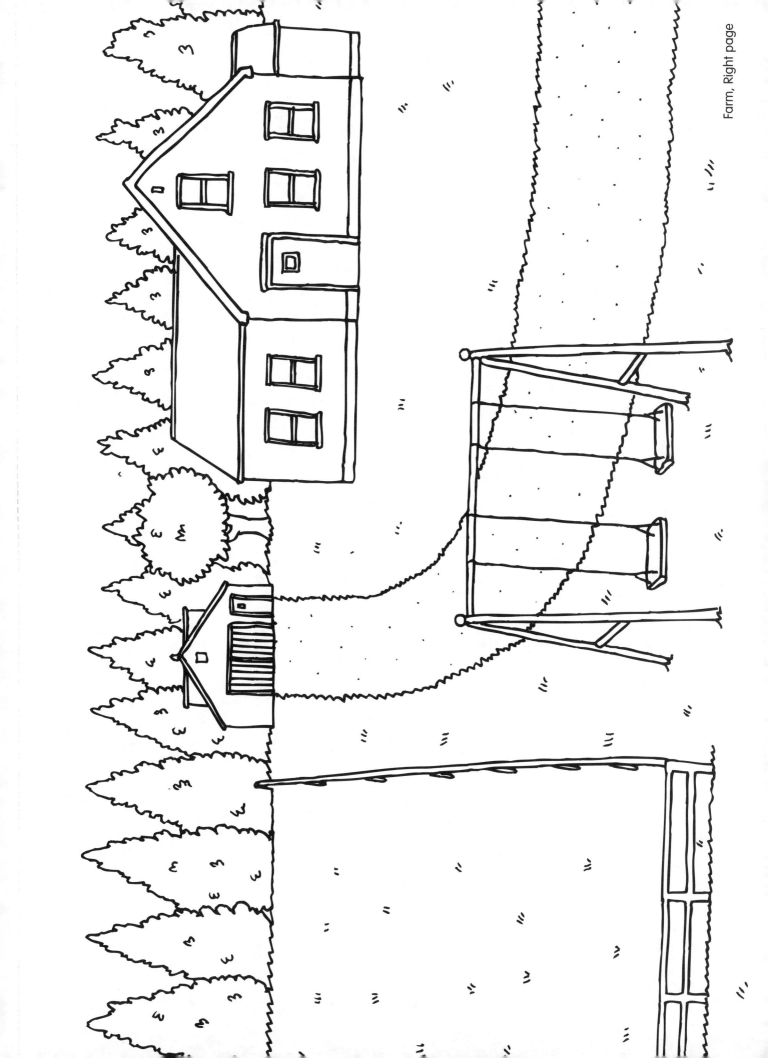

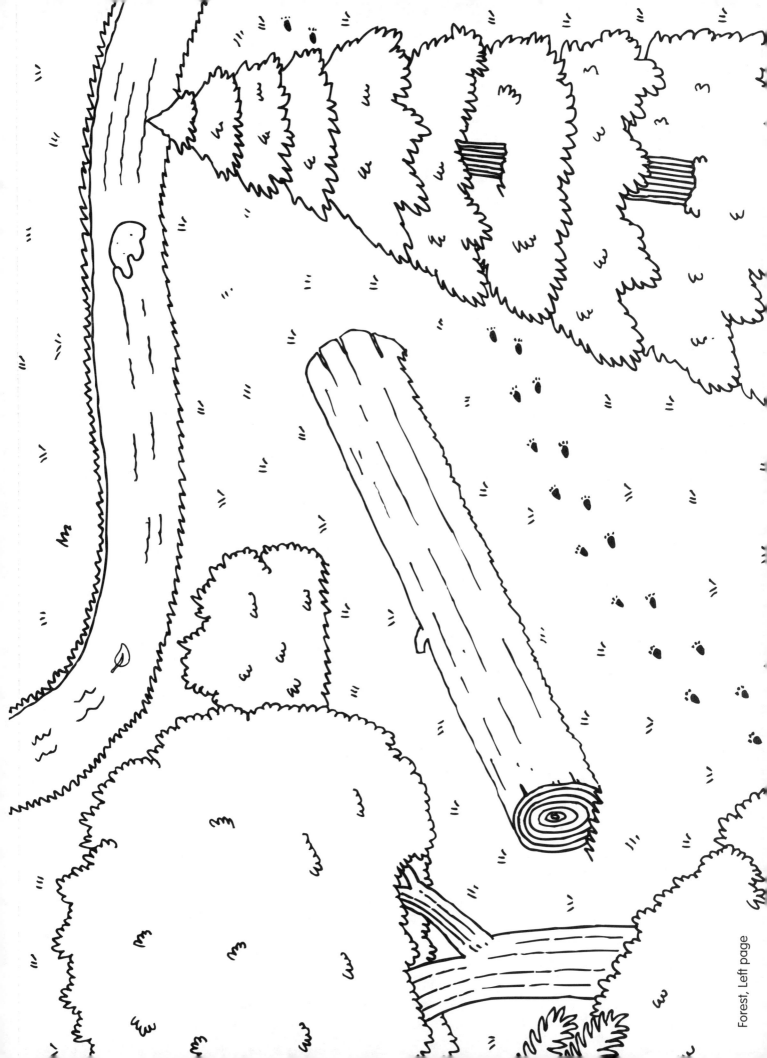

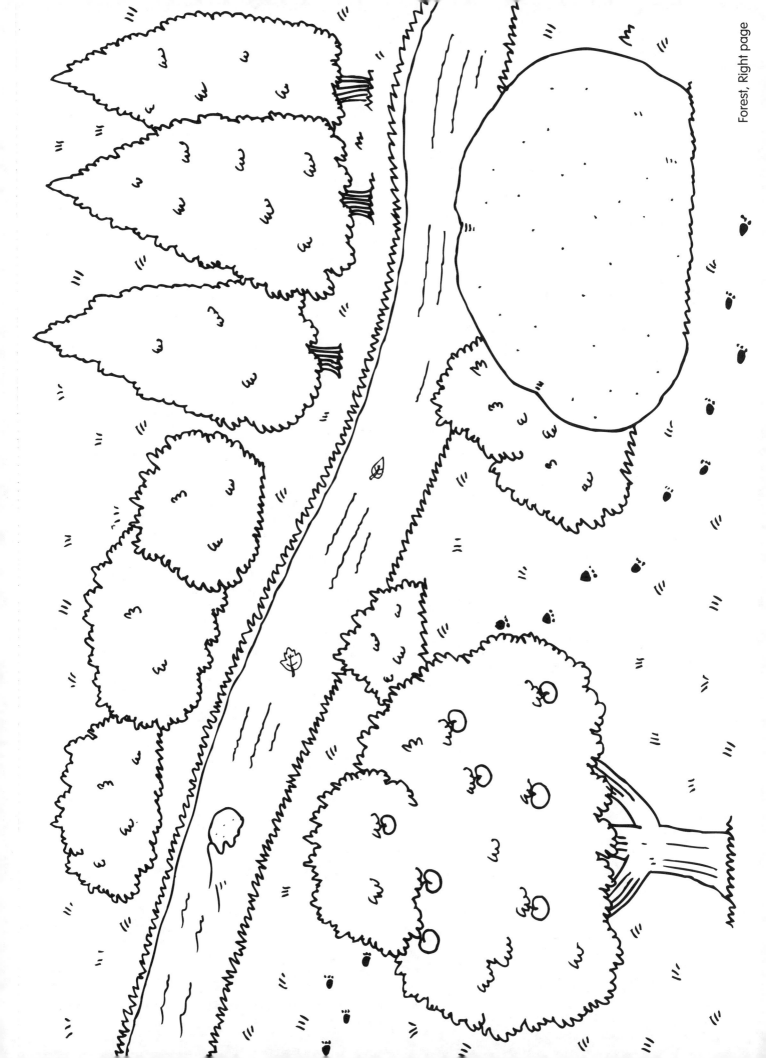

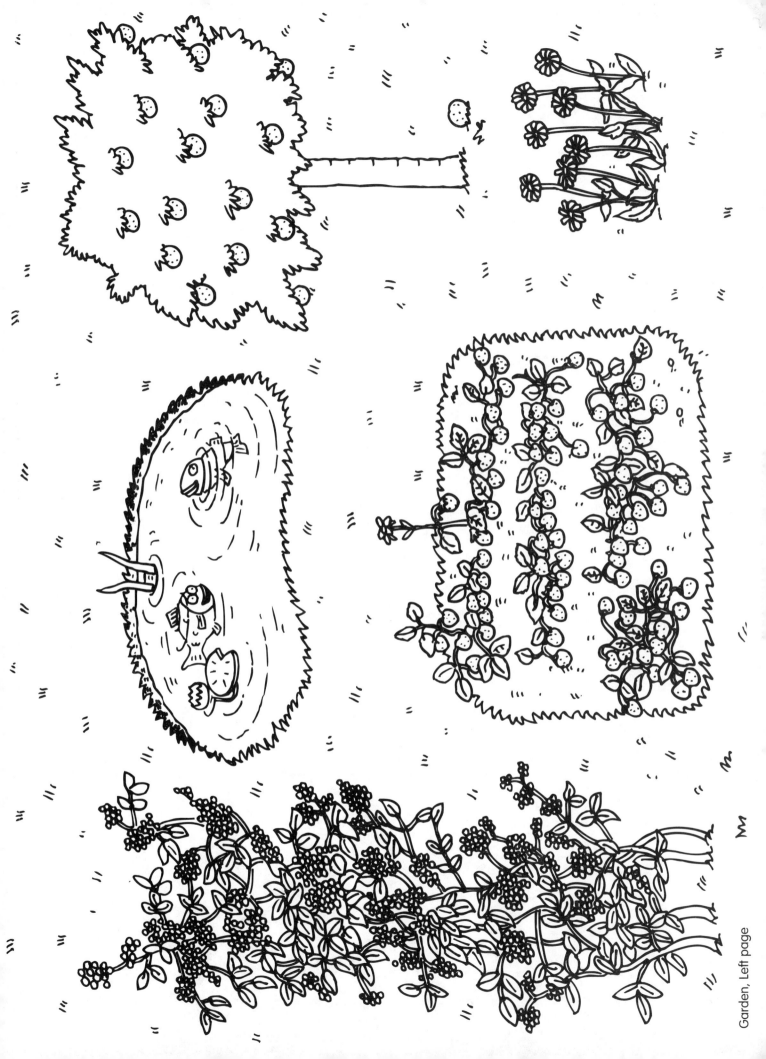

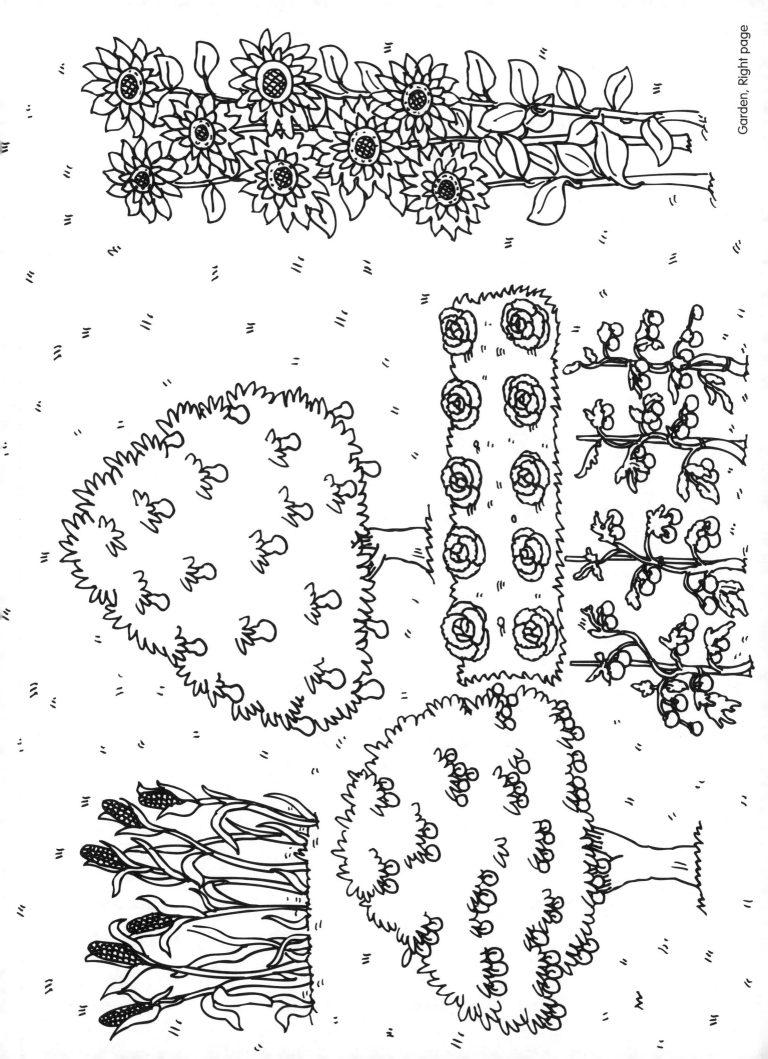

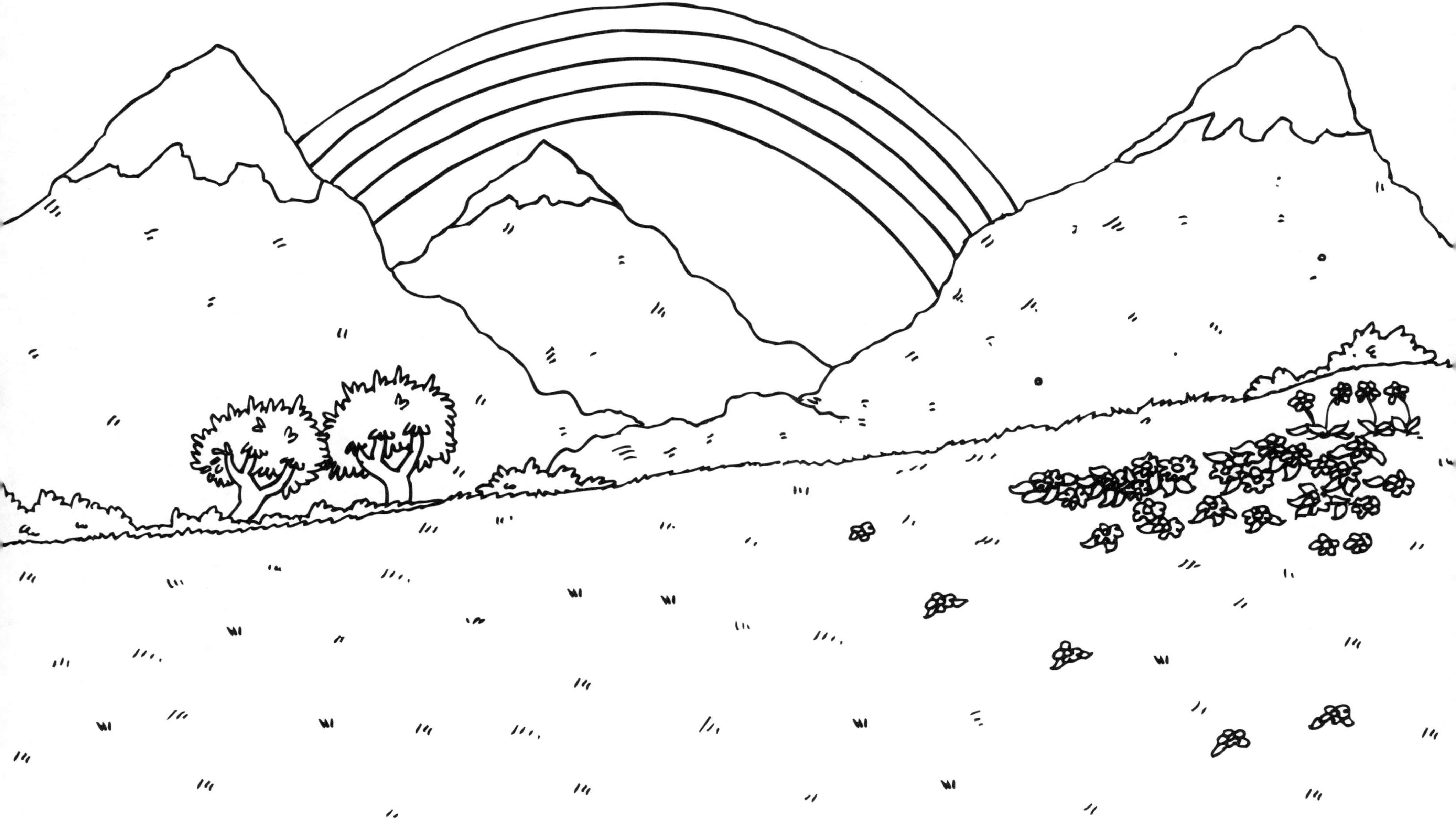

Mountain Meadow, Left page

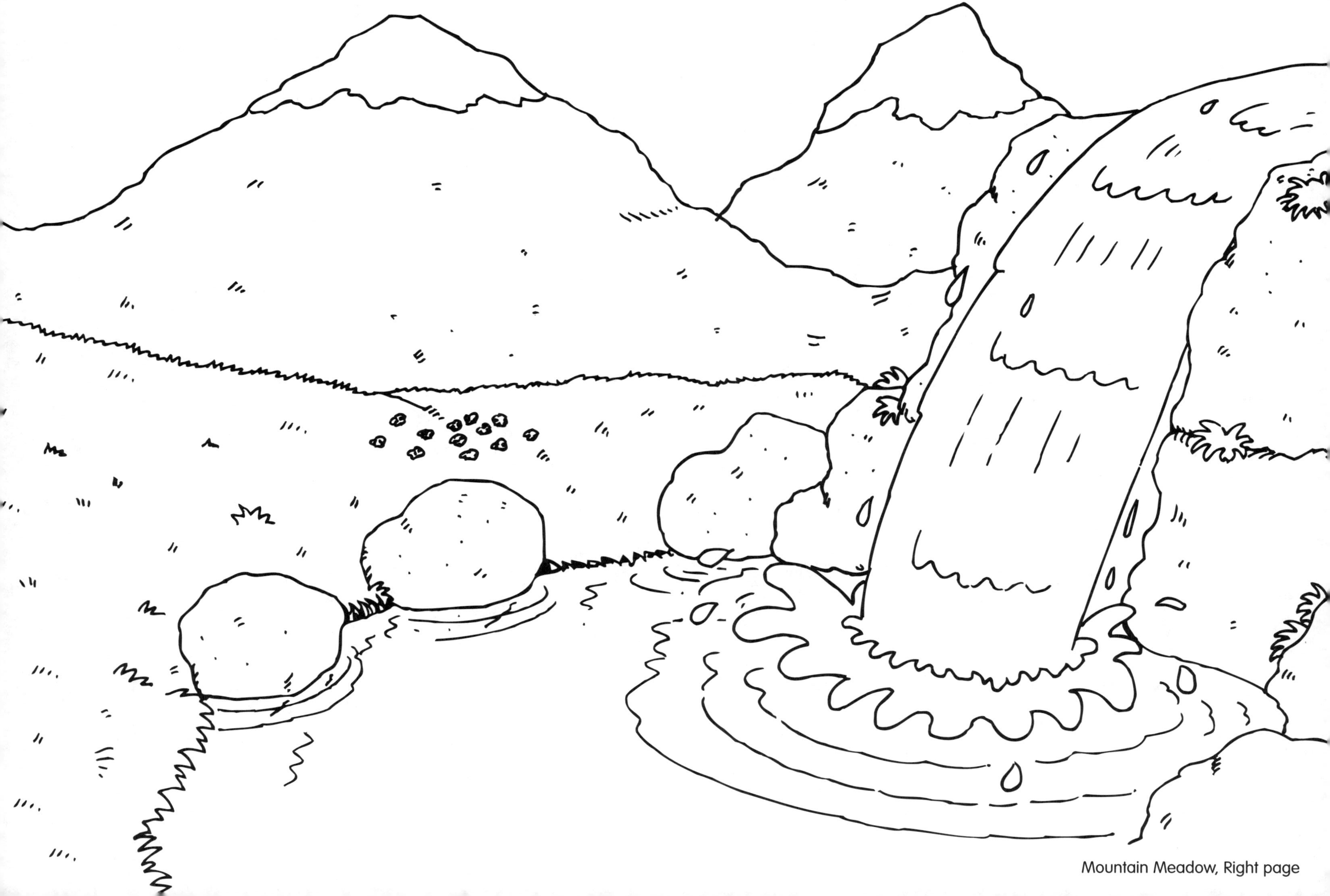

Mountain Meadow, Right page

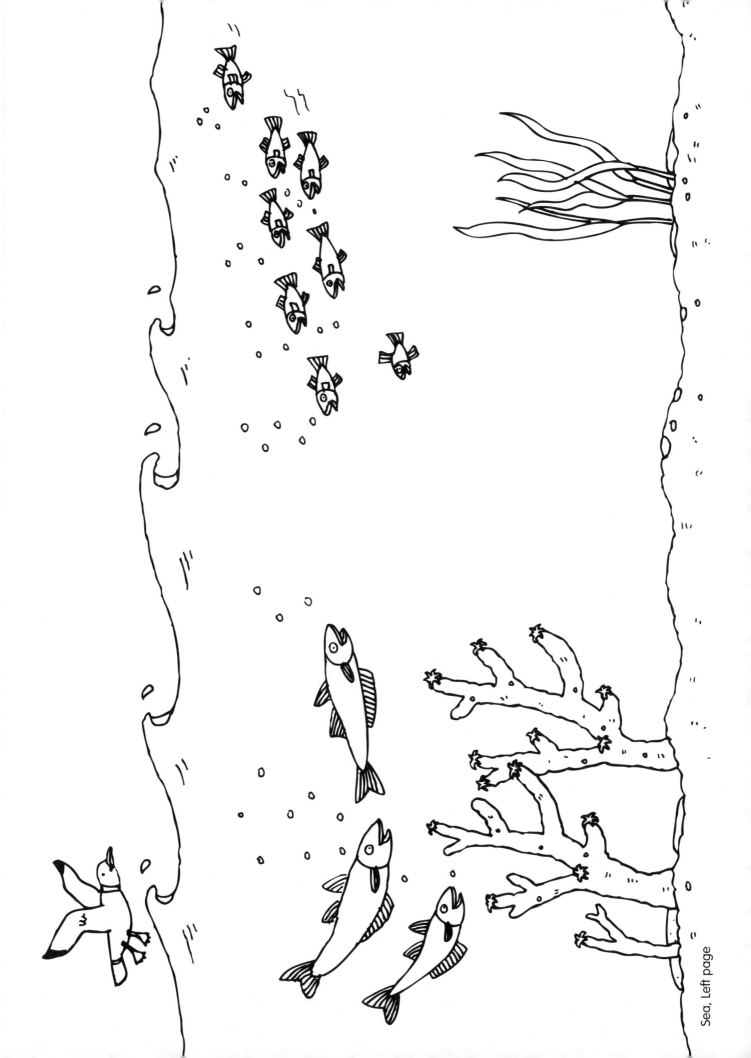

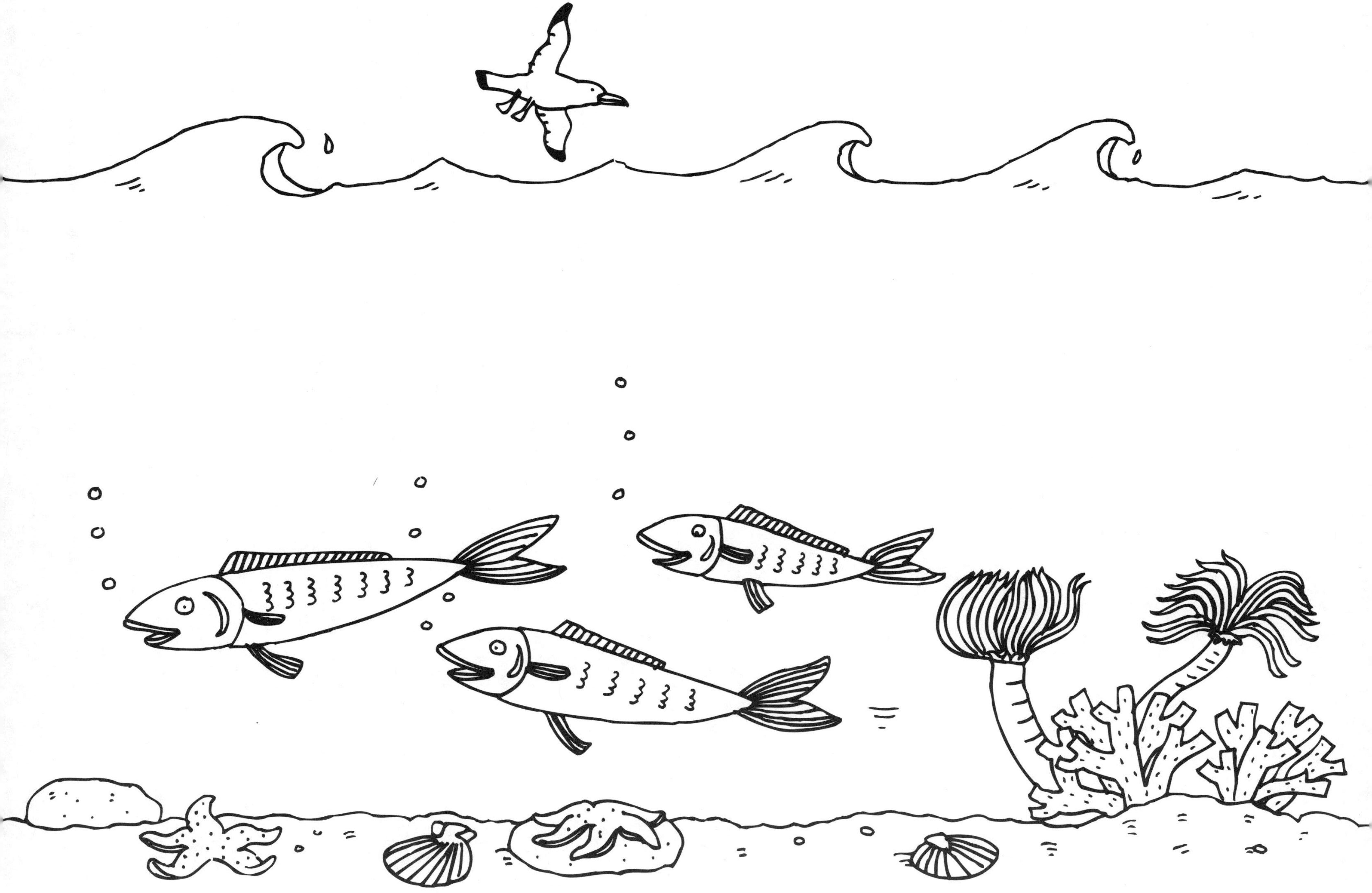

Sea, Right page

Domino Play

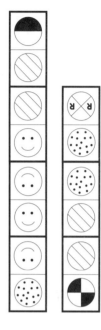

Children love dominoes, but traditional dominoes require significant math skills and pattern recognition abilities and come in large sets. The games and sets in this book fit young children: there are fewer dominoes than in regular sets, and pattern recognition is by looking at pictures rather than by counting a number of figures. The activity list includes teamwork games and open-ended creative activities which offer fun possibilities for each of your children.

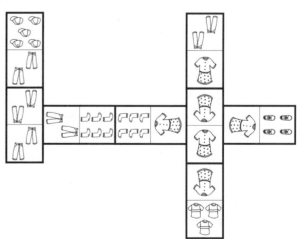

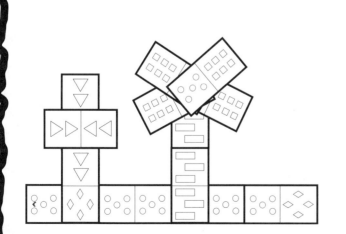

HOW to Prepare the Domino Play

☼ Photocopy the pages onto white and/or colored card stock or copier paper.

☼ Laminate pages or cover with clear Con-Tact paper.

☼ Cut pages apart along the heavy lines using a paper cutter or scissors.

☼ For a handy collection of games and activities, save each set of prepared materials with a copy of the game and and its directions in an envelope, folder or resealable plastic bag.

Basic Dominoes

Materials: One set of dominoes (choose from pp. 243-257; prepare as instructed on p. 236).

Procedure: Children sit in a circle. Mix dominoes and place five dominoes faceup in front of each child. The remaining dominoes are left facedown, unstacked near the players. First player places one domino in the middle of the circle. The next player places a domino with a matching end next to the first domino. If a player does not have a domino with a matching end, then the player draws a domino from the extra dominoes. If player does not draw a domino with a matching end, next player takes turn. If there are no dominoes left to draw, then that player's turn is skipped. (Note: Doubles are placed perpendicular to other dominoes and each end or side of a double may be added to.) Play continues until players have run out of dominoes, no one can make a play or as time and interest allow.

Variation: When a player does not have a domino with a matching end, the next person plays; there is no drawing.

✿ **Group Size:** One to four players

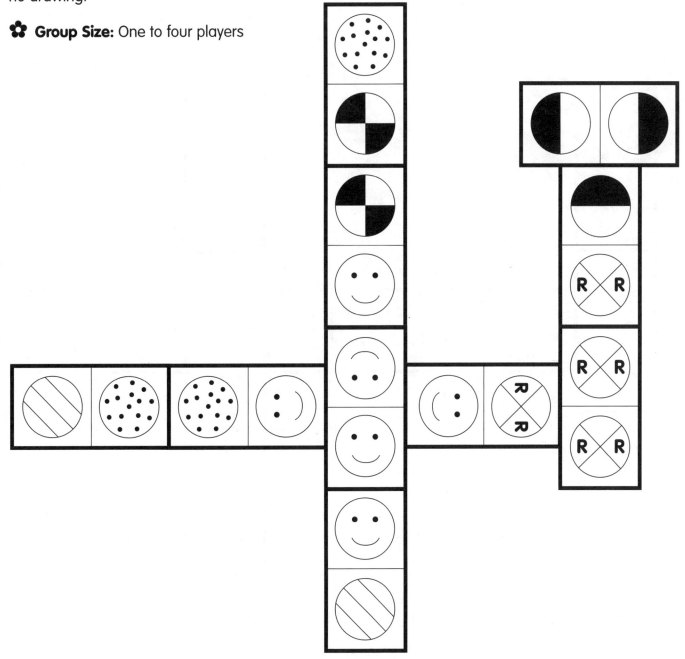

Double Doubles

Materials: One set of dominoes (choose from pp. 243-257; prepare as instructed on p. 236).

Procedure: Children sit in a circle. Mix dominoes and place an equal number of dominoes faceup in front of each child. Any extra dominoes are set aside for the rest of the game. First player places one domino in the middle of the circle. The next player places a domino with a matching end next to the first domino. If a player does not have a domino with a matching end, then the next person plays. Every time a player plays a double domino, he or she may place a second domino, too. Players continue to place dominoes next to a domino with a matching end. (Note: Doubles are placed perpendicular to other dominoes and each end or side of a double may be added to.) Play continues until players have run out of dominoes, no one can make a play or as time and interest allow.

❀ **Group Size:** Two to four players

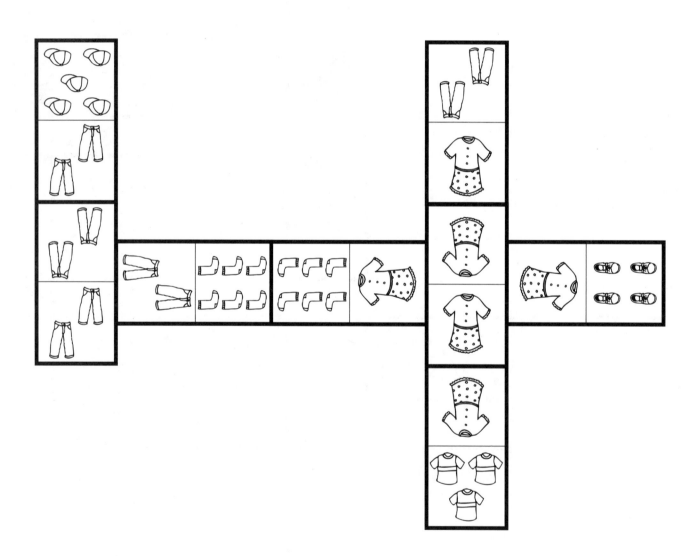

Racing Trains

Materials: One set of dominoes (choose from pp. 243-257; prepare as instructed on p. 236).

Procedure: Children sit in a circle. Mix dominoes and place an equal number of dominoes faceup in front of each child. Set aside extra dominoes. First player places one domino in the middle of the circle. The next player places a domino parallel to the first one, approximately 2 inches (5 cm) from it. The next player places a domino with a matching end next to the first domino. If a player does not have a domino with a matching end, then the next person plays.

Players continue to place dominoes next to an end domino with a matching end to create two "trains." Play continues until players have run out of dominoes, no one can make a play or as time and interest allow.

✿ **Group Size:** One to four players

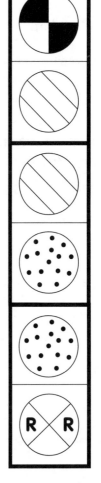

Solo

Materials: One set of dominoes for each child (choose from pp. 243-257; prepare as instructed on p. 236).

Procedure: Give one set of dominoes to each child. The child, at his or her own pace, places dominoes on a flat surface, matching the ends. Dominoes may be placed in a straight line, an L or a crossword puzzle pattern. Play continues until all dominoes have been played or as time and interest allow.

Variation: Child lays matching ends on top of each other and in any direction.

✿ **Group Size:** One or more players

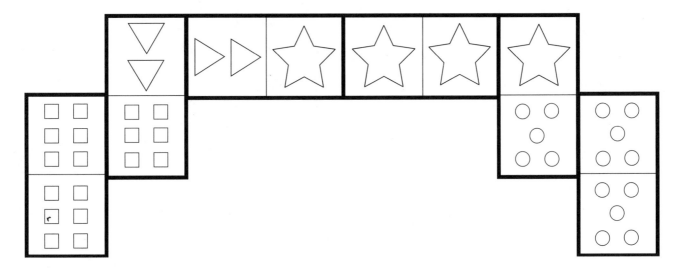

Spokes

Materials: One set of dominoes (choose from pp. 243-257; prepare as instructed on p. 236).

Procedure: Children sit in a circle. Mix dominoes and place an equal number of dominoes faceup in front of each child. Set aside extra dominoes. Help one child place a double domino in the middle of the circle. The next player places a domino with a matching end touching an end or side of the first domino (see sketch). If a player does not have a domino with a matching end, the next player takes a turn. Play continues until players have run out of dominoes, no one can make a play or as time and interest allow. (Note: Players may build up to four spokes from the first domino played. All dominoes, including doubles, are played in straight lines.)

Variation: Use two copies of the same set (allows up to six players).

❀ **Group Size:** Two to four players

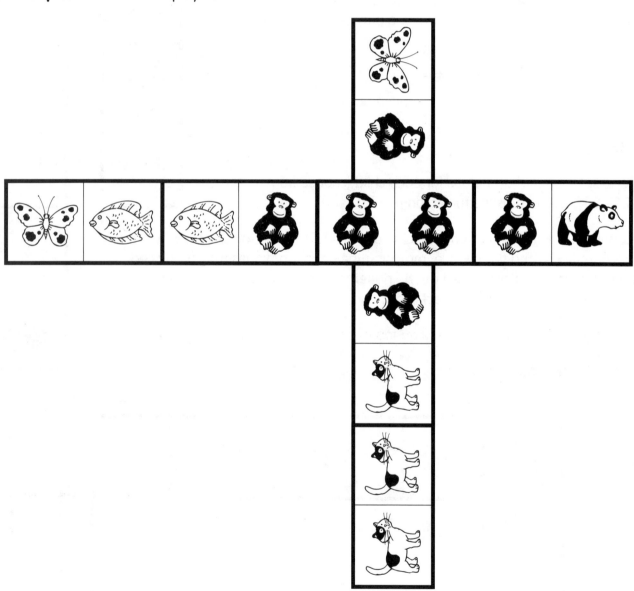

Mosaic

Materials: One set of dominoes for each child or for every two children (choose from pp. 243-257; prepare as instructed on p. 236).

Procedure: Give one set of dominoes to each child or each pair of children. The child (or children) places the dominoes to create a design of his or her own choosing. For example, one child may place several dominoes to form a diagonal shape while another child may place dominoes in the shape of a house or a tree. Play continues until all dominoes have been placed or as time and interest allow.

✿ **Group Size:** One or two players

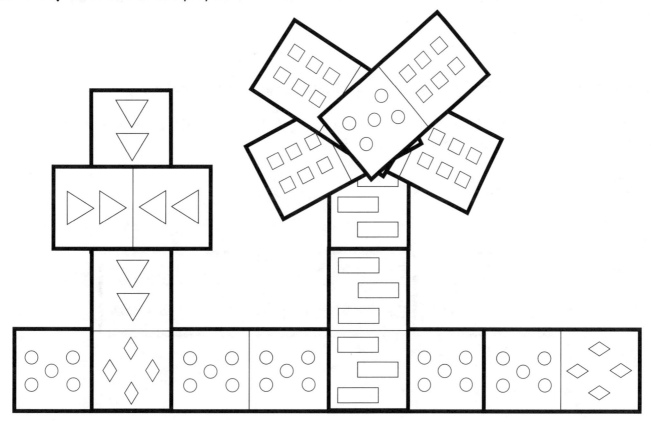

Game for Older Children

Sevens

Materials: Clothing or Shape Dominoes (pp. 251-253 or 255-257; prepare as instructed on p. 236).

Procedure: Children sit in a circle. Mix dominoes and place five dominoes faceup in front of each child. The remaining dominoes are left facedown, unstacked near the players. First player places one domino in the middle of the circle. The next player places a domino whose end adds up to seven with one end of the first domino (see sketch). If the player does not have a domino whose end will add up to seven with one end of the first domino, the player draws from the facedown dominoes until one is drawn that can be played. If there are no dominoes left to draw, then that player's turn is skipped. Play continues until players have run out of dominoes, no one can make a play or as time and interest allow.

Variations:

• If only two or three are playing, players may start with seven dominoes apiece.

• A domino with two ends that add up to seven (6+1, 5+2 or 4+3) is called a super seven, and it may be placed beside any other domino.

✿ **Group Size:** Two to four players

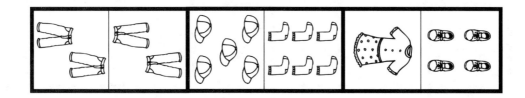

Animal
Dominoes

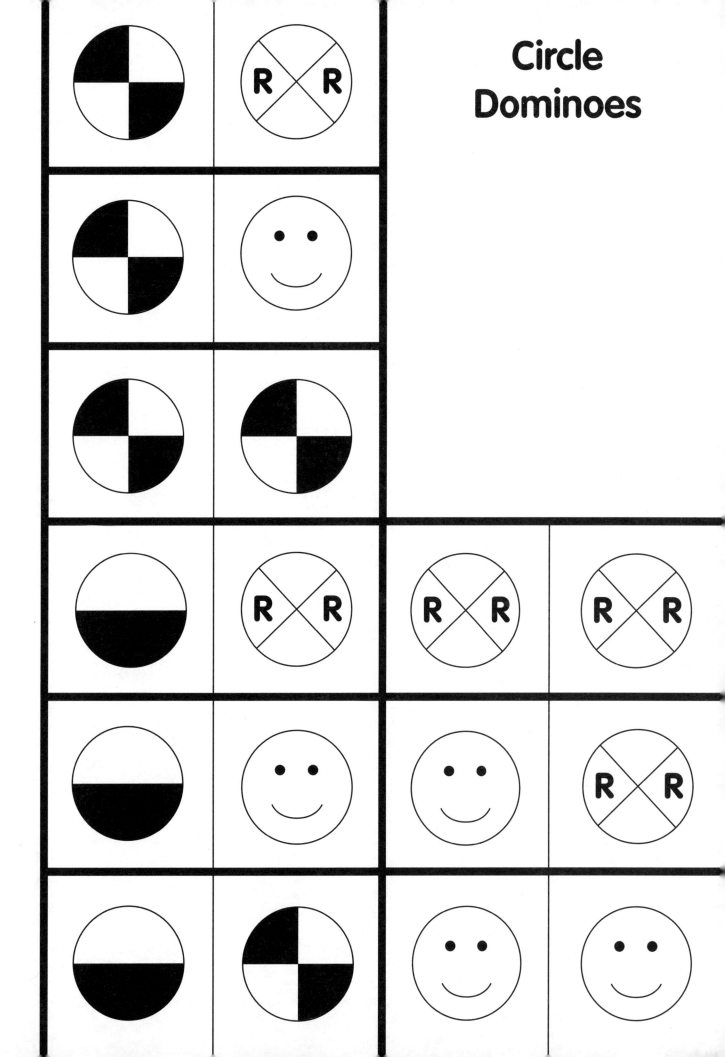

Circle Dominoes

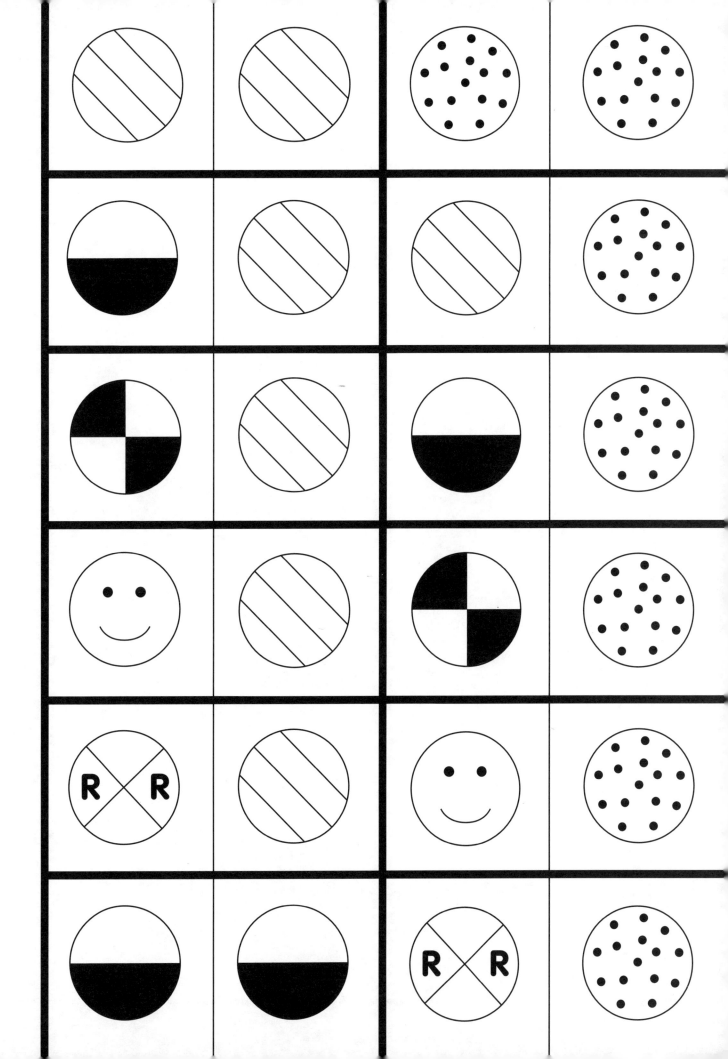

Clothing Dominoes

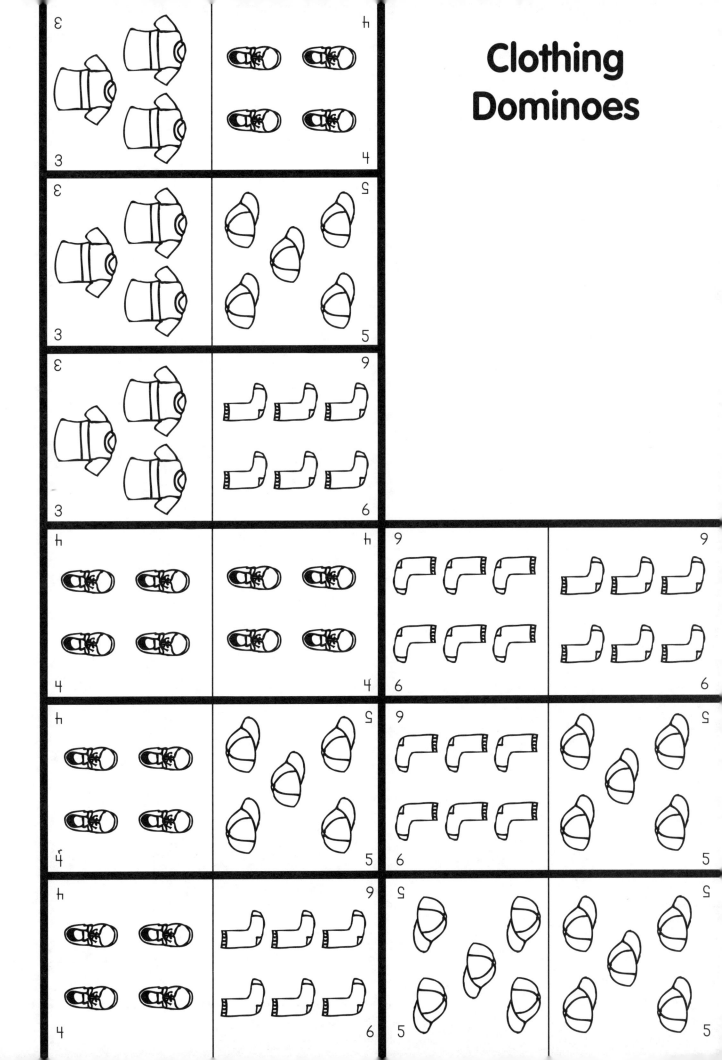

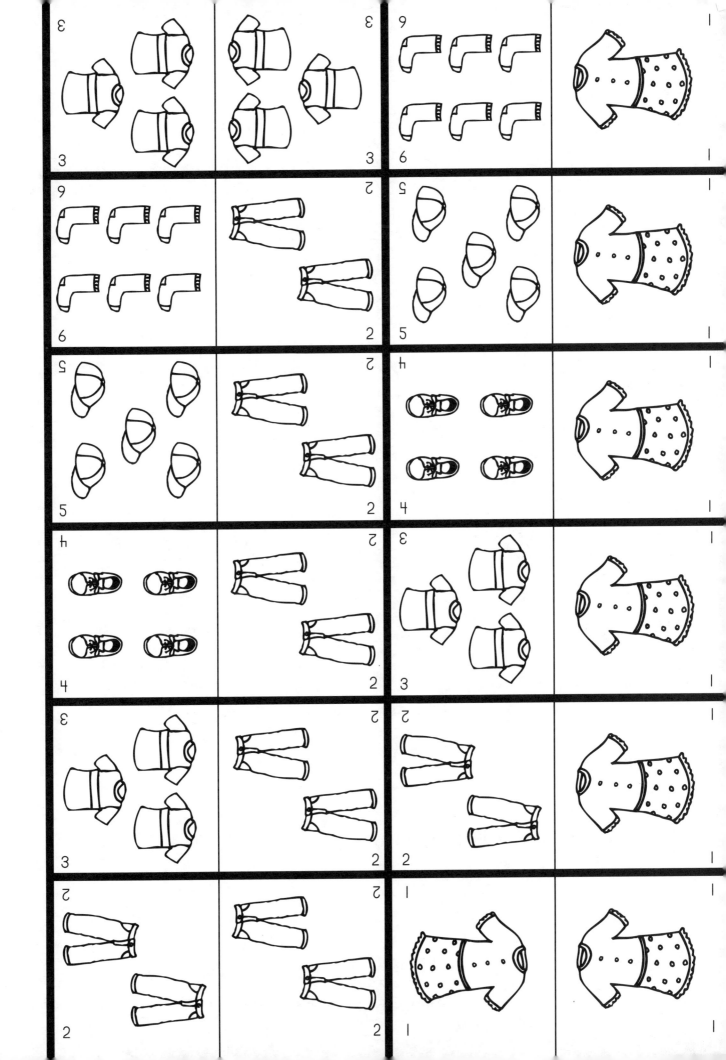

Shape
Dominoes

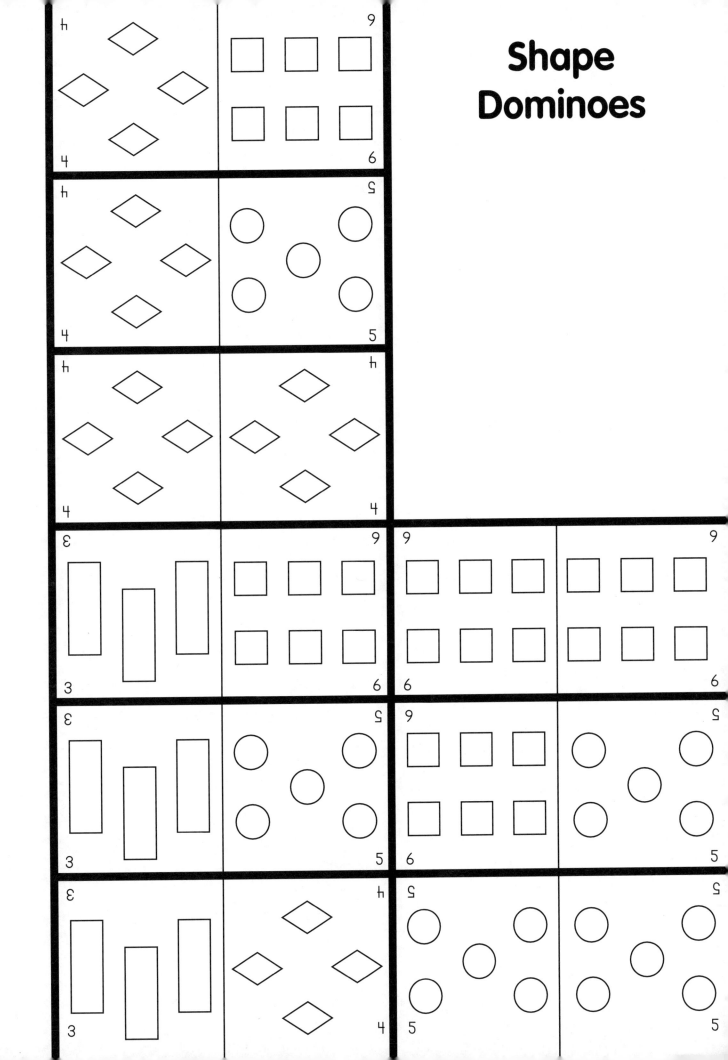

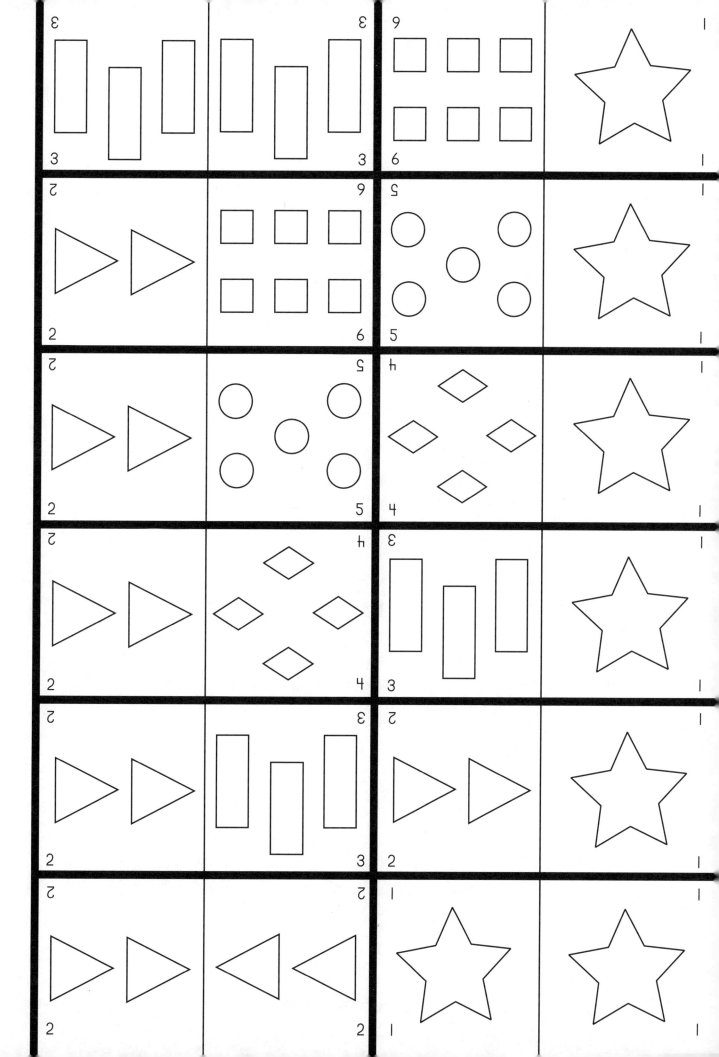

Big Bible Learning Fun!

The Big Book of Kindergarten Puzzles
A full year's worth of fun Bible puzzles—mazes, dot-to-dots, letters, shapes and more! Bible story and verse puzzles to go with every lesson! Reproducible.
Manual • 216p
ISBN 08307.27574

The Big Book of Instant Activities
Over 100 fun, simple activities to help teachers with transitions, regaining attention and just having fun! Reproducible.
Manual • 176p
ISBN 08307.26624

The Big Book of Christian Growth
Discipling made easy! 306 discussion cards based on Bible passages, and 75 games and activities for preteens. Reproducible.
Manual •176p
ISBN 08307.25865

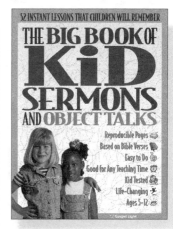

The Big Book of Kid Sermons and Object Talks
Relate Bible principles to young lives with object talks. Ages 5 to 12.
Manual •112p
ISBN 08307.25164

The Big Book of Service Projects
Over 80 reproducible service projects. Many can be completed in class!
Manual •176p
ISBN 08307.26330

Read-Aloud Story and Activity Book, Vol. 1
Reproducible coloring activities and contemporary stories about Bible truths.
Complete instructions and questions on every page.
Manual • 222p
ISBN 08307.27701

Bible Verse Coloring Pages
Bible learning with crayons. Includes 116 verses in both *NIV* and *KJV* translations. Reproducible.
Manual • 240p
SPCN 25116.06720

Bible Verse Coloring Pages #2
Reproducible coloring pictures for children ages 5 to 8. Includes both *NIV* and *KJV* verses.
Manual • 216p
ISBN 08307.25857

Available from your Gospel Light supplier.
www.gospellight.com

Gospel Light
God's Word for a Kid's World!

Smart Resources for Your Children's Ministry

Sunday School Smart Pages
Training, inspiration, materials, quick solutions and more for teaching ages 2 to 12.
Reproducible
Manual • ISBN 08307.15215

Sunday School Promo Pages
Resources and advice to recruit teachers, gain church support, increase attendance and more.
Reproducible
Manual • ISBN 08307.15894

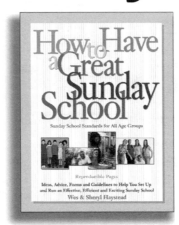

How to Have a Great Sunday School
Ideas, advice, forms and guidelines to help you set up and run an effective, efficient and exciting Sunday School at every age level.
Reproducible
Manual • ISBN 08307.18265

The Big Book of Bible Crafts
Fun for Sunday School, Christian Schools, Day Care, Home Schools, Cell Groups, Midweek Programs, and Family Time. Ages 3 to 12.
Reproducible
Manual • ISBN 08307.25733

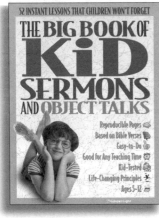

The Big Book of Kid Sermons and Object Talks
52 instant lessons! Everyday objects are used to illustrate life-changing principles of the Bible for kids to understand. Ages 5 to 12.
Reproducible
Manual • ISBN 08307.25164

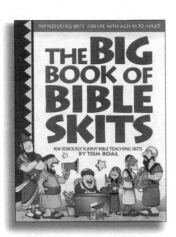

The Big Book of Bible Skits
104 seriously funny Bible teaching skits. Includes discussion questions. Ages 10 to adult.
Reproducible
Manual • ISBN 08307.19164

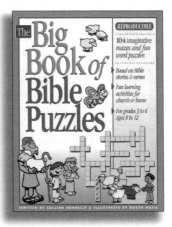

The Big Book of Bible Puzzles
104 imaginative mazes and fun word puzzles based on Bible stories and verses. Fun learning activites for grades 3 to 6. Ages 8 to 12.
Reproducible
Manual • ISBN 08307.25423

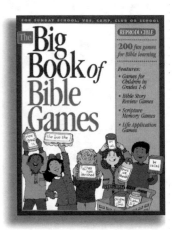

The Big Book of Bible Games
200 fun games that teach Bible concepts and life application. Ages 5 to 12.
Reproducible
Manual • ISBN 08307.18214

Get All the Bible Fun Songs Music on Video, CD, Cassette and DVD!

Volume 1: God's Plan
Video • Approx. 28 minutes
UPC 607135.004592
CD
UPC 607135.005018
Cassette
UPC 607135.005001

Volume 2: God's Power
Video • Approx. 25 minutes
UPC 607135.004608
CD
UPC 607135.005032
Cassette
UPC 607135.005025

Volume 3: God's Protection
Video • Approx. 28 minutes
UPC 607135.004714
CD
UPC 607135.005056
Cassette
UPC 607135.005063

Volume 4: God's Praise
Video • Approx. 25 minutes
UPC 607135.004998
CD
UPC 607135.005070
Cassette
UPC 607135.005087

Volume 5: God's Promises
Video • Approx. 28 minutes
UPC 607135.005773
CD
UPC 607135.005803
Cassette
UPC 607135.005797

Volume 6: God's Presence
Video • Approx. 28 minutes
UPC 607135.005780
CD
UPC 607135.005827
Cassette
UPC 607135.005810

Volume 7: Kids on the Rock
Video • Approx. 30 minutes
UPC 607135.006152
CD
UPC 607135.006329
Cassette
UPC 607135.006336

Volumes 1 & 2
DVD • Approx.
50 minutes
UPC 607135.006114

Volumes 3 & 4
DVD • Approx.
50 minutes
UPC 607135.006121

Volumes 5 & 6
DVD • Approx.
45 minutes
UPC 607135.006350

Available at your local Christian bookstore.
www.gospellight.com

Pulse
GOD'S WORD
FOR A JR. HIGH WORLD

Young people between the ages of 11 and 14 are the most open to who Jesus is and what a life with Him offers. Reach them with Pulse—designed especially for them!

Throughout the cutting-edge series, 3 categories of study help junior highers understand and apply God's Word in their lives: Biblical, Life Issues, Discipleship.

Connect with junior highers—get all 24 Pulse studies!

#13 Peer Pressure
ISBN 08307.25490

#14 The Early Church
ISBN 08307.25504

#15 Worship
ISBN 08307.25512

#16 Changes
ISBN 08307.25520

#17 Faith
ISBN 08307.25539

#18 The Great Commission
ISBN 08307.25547

#1 Christianity: the Basics
ISBN 08307.24079

#2 Prayer
ISBN 08307.24087

#3 Friends
ISBN 08307.24192

#4 Teachings of Jesus
ISBN 08307.24095

#5 Followers of Christ
ISBN 08307.24117

#6 Teens of the Bible
ISBN 08307. 24125

#7 Life at School
ISBN 08307.25083

#8 Miracles of Jesus
ISBN 08307.25091

#9 Home and Family
ISBN 08307.25105

#10 Genesis
ISBN 08307.25113

#11 Fruit of the Spirit
ISBN 08307.25474

#12 Feelings & Emotions
ISBN 08307.25482

#19 Love, Sex & Dating
ISBN 08307.25555

#20 What the Bible Is All About
ISBN 08307.25563

#21 Self-Image
ISBN 08307.25571

#22 Spiritual Gifts
ISBN 08307.25598

#23 Hear My Voice
ISBN 08307.25601

#24 Do Unto Others
ISBN 08307.25628

Available at your local Christian bookstore
www.gospellight.com

 **Gospel Light**

041633

Turn Good Volunteers into Great Teachers

Smart Teacher Training Videos are the smart, easy way to recruit, train and motivate teachers! Developed by Sunday School authorities Wes and Sheryl Haystead, each video includes expert advice, live classroom demonstrations and answers to the most common questions asked by teachers.

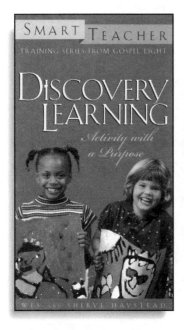

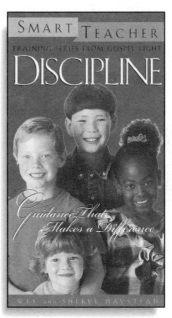

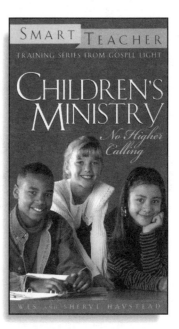

Discovery Learning: Activity with a Purpose
Guide children in the joy of discovering foundational truths for a lifetime of learning.
Video • UPC 607135.003601

Bible Skills for Better Teaching: Helping Kids Make the Connection
Practical ways to build interest, develop Bible skills and make the Bible relevant to kids.
Video • UPC 607135.003588

Discipline: Guidance that Makes a Difference
Behavior challenges give teachers opportunities to demonstrate God's love and forgiveness, and help kids learn to do what's right.
Video • UPC 607135.003618

Children's Ministry: No Higher Calling
Challenge your teachers to consider the value Christ places on children and the astounding benefits ministry to children brings.
Video • UPC 607135.003595

Available from your Gospel Light supplier.
www.gospellight.com

Gospel Light